PRIDE OF THE DONS

Pride of the Dons

The untold story of the men and women who made the Gothenburg Greats

Derek Niven

Published in paperback in 2024 by Corkerhill Press
Published in eBook in 2023 by Corkerhill Press
Copyright © Derek Niven 2024

Derek Niven has asserted his right to be identified as the author of this work in accordance with the Copyright, Designs and Patents Act 1988

Front cover illustrations by Wheech © 2024

ISBN paperback: 978-1-7393929-6-3
ISBN ebook: 978-1-7393929-7-0

All rights reserved. No part of this publication, including the cover illustrations, may be reproduced, stored in a retrieval system, or transmitted in any form or by means, electronic, photocopying, recording or otherwise, without the prior permission of the copyright owner.

All characters and events in this publication are based on factual, historical and genealogical research recorded in the public domain. Any errors in the research are purely accidental and entirely the ownership of the author and all research has been carried out in good faith.

A CIP catalogue copy of this book can be found at the British Library in London, the National Library of Scotland and various University libraries in UK and Ireland.

Published with the help of Indie Authors World

Acknowledgements

The author wishes to acknowledge his Indie Authors World partners Sinclair and Kim Macleod's valued assistance in publishing this series of footballing history books. The author also thanks his editor Gillian Murphy for her usual ardent and studious efforts. Many thanks to my great friends John Steele and Robin Dale, who initially encouraged me to 'kick on' with this idea of a book series. A special thanks to the Dim Dam Tea Estate in India for their research and memories of the Cooper family who lived and worked there. As with my previous publications, thanks also to the late Sir Dirk Bogarde, actor and author, for the pseudonym and to our old alumni Allan Glen's School for the unrivalled education.

Finally, without my wife Linda's unswerving love, support and patience, this book would never have seen the light of day.

PRIDE OF THE DONS

"There is nothing impossible to him who will try."
– Alexander the Great

Contents

Preface

Chapter 1: Jim Leighton
Chapter 2: Doug Rougvie
Chapter 3: John McMaster
Chapter 4: Neale Cooper
Chapter 5: Alex McLeish
Chapter 6: Willie Miller (c)
Chapter 7: Gordon Strachan
Chapter 8: Neil Simpson
Chapter 9: Mark McGhee
Chapter 10: Eric Black
Chapter 11: Peter Weir
Chapter 12: Stuart Kennedy
Chapter 13: Bryan Gunn
Chapter 14: Andy Watson
Chapter 15: John Hewitt
Chapter 16: Ian Angus
Chapter 17: Sir Alex Ferguson

Conclusion

References

About the Author

PRIDE OF THE DONS

Preface

The casual reader may think this sixth book in the Pride Series is about football. On the contrary, this book is the continuation of fickle fate and destiny. It examines the chance accumulation of fateful meetings and unions between men and women from the early 19th century. This culminated in the procreation of a remarkable group of young men, who wrote themselves into the history books 40 years ago. It is about men and women who were born more than 60 years before the formation of a new association football club in 1903 in the north east city of Aberdeen, which eventually grew into the world-renowned Aberdeen Football Club. These were people who were brought together by destiny, having no idea that one day their descendants would be immortalised over a hundred years after their own births in the mid-19th century.

Aberdeen FC was formed in 1903, the amalgamation of three teams in the city at that time, including an older Aberdeen FC (1881-1903). As a small provincial club, Aberdeen rarely challenged for honours until the post-war decade, when they won each of the major Scottish trophies under manager Dave Halliday. However, the halcyon days at the club were to come in the 1980s with the signing of the Don's new young manager Alex Ferguson. At that time, the city of Aberdeen was booming with the North Sea oil industry and money was pouring into the city. This became the era of the "New Firm", overshadowing the "Old Firm" rivalry of Rangers and Celtic, when Ferguson vied with his great rival Jim McLean at Dundee United for success in Scotland and Europe.

In an incredible run of success, Aberdeen won three Scottish League titles, four Scottish Cups, a Scottish League Cup and the Drybrough Cup. The pinnacle of success came in 1983 when they won the European Cup Winners' Cup, the last Scottish team to achieve that feat, and a European Super Cup. Aberdeen remains the only Scottish team to win two major UEFA European trophies.

On a very damp evening, which required a pre-match pitch inspection after a day of torrential rain, on 11 May 1983 in the Nya Ullevi Stadium in Gothenburg, Sweden, sixteen young Scotsmen playing for Aberdeen created football history by beating the mighty Spanish side Real Madrid 2–1 to lift the European Cup Winner's Cup. It was an extraordinary feat for a small provincial club to defeat the Spanish giants of European football. My railway colleague and friend David Chester and my brother James McGee, although both Glasgow Rangers fans, made the trip to Gothenburg to see Scottish footballing history enacted.

Looking at the exorbitantly paid international players developed nowadays at Barcelona, Real Madrid, Chelsea, Manchester United and Bayern Munich football clubs, who compete for European trophies, it can be quickly realised that never again will a team of working-class local lads win such a coveted trophy. Billions are now spent on Europe's most sought-after awards. Soon after leaving Aberdeen for even greater success at Manchester United, Ferguson realised that building new sides for European success would require signing players from across the international spectrum, the young Portuguese Cristiano Ronaldo being Ferguson's greatest signing.

In 2023, the Gothenburg Greats celebrated the 40th anniversary of their landmark victory and Aberdeen FC marked its 120th anniversary. Much was rewritten about that famous 1982–83 campaign culminating in the final game at Nya Ullevi Stadium. Minute details documented the momentous game starting with Eric Black's seventh minute strike from a Strachan corner. However, Real Madrid responded quickly in the increasingly muddy conditions. Following a short pass back by McLeish, which stuck in the mud, goalkeeper Leighton gave away a penalty, scored by Juanito.

The match was tied 1–1 at full-time and it went into extra time. In the 112th minute, Peter Weir passed to Mark McGhee and his measured cross was headed in by substitute John Hewitt for the winning goal. All of that detail, eagerly awaited by Aberdeen fans around the globe, was written more succinctly than myself, penned by authors and sports journalists who are football men.

The author is a professional genealogist and member of ASGRA. The reader may ask what brought a professional genealogist to want to write the family histories of the Aberdeen heroes. It began with his support for Celtic FC.

On the evening of 25 May 1967 his mother took him, aged eleven, up to his Gran McCue's high-rise flat in Pollokshaws on the south side of Glasgow. His grandmother Annie Collie was Protestant, but his grandfather Frank McCue and his son, Uncle Jim, were Catholic. While his mother chatted away to her mother Annie, we 'men' sat enthralled watching the historic game unfold on the small Phillips black and white television. At the age of eleven, he was too young to travel to football games on his own, so he did not immediately become a Celtic fan.

Fate lent a hand.

His father Archie was an ardent Rangers supporter and he wanted him to follow the Teddy Bears. To that end, on 7 September 1969, his father took him to Ibrox Park to watch Rangers face Polish side Gornik Zabrze in a UEFA Cup Winners' Cup second leg match. Rangers trailed 3–1 from the first leg, but the manager Davie White's side was optimistic overcoming that score in the return match on home turf. That optimism was totally dispelled that damp evening when Rangers were beaten by another 3–1 defeat, beaten 6–2 by Gornik. The defeat ended Davie White's managerial career, but as the father and son trudged despondently back from Ibrox Park to Corkerhill, Archie uttered these fateful words, "I'll never be back at Ibrox again." Although he have a copy of the match programme, given to him on his retirement from the rail industry in 2007 by his great railway colleague, DJ Steeley, it seems to serve as a reminder of his father's dismissive words and that Rangers was not the team for him at that point in his young life.

PRIDE OF THE DONS

Celtic continued to dominate Scottish football. They were on course for a record-breaking 'nine-in-a-row' league championship title and another final appearance in the European Cup against the Dutch team Feyenoord in 1970. He decided to support Celtic. His Protestant father Archie had no objections, although he would rather have seen his son go to Ibrox. Two of his younger brothers, James and David, became ardent Rangers' supporters. In fact, the author was the only one in a family of eight who did not support Rangers.

It was that Celtic support dating back to 1967 that inspired me to write this book. Pride of the Lions celebrates the Lisbon Lions not from a footballing perspective but from a genealogical, familial, religious and social history perspective.

The second book in the series, published in 2018, was Pride of the Jocks. This book celebrates the 16 greatest Scottish football managers, such as Busby, Shankly, Stein and Sir Alex Ferguson. It does so from the perspective of the men and women who made them genealogically. It also includes Gordon Strachan's family history, who played in the Gothenburg final.

The third book in the series, Pride of the Bears, published in 2020, tells the family histories of the men and women who created the Rangers team that won the European Cup Winners' Cup in 1972.

The fourth book in the series, Pride of the Hearts, published in 2021, tells the extraordinarily poignant and tragic histories of the 16 Hearts players who enlisted in McCrae's Battalion during the Great War.

The fifth book in the series, Pride of the Three Lions, published in 2023, tells the histories behind the England team that beat West Germany 4–2 at Wembley in 1966.

This book series shows that even in greatness, we are, as we say in Scotland, "a' Jock Tamson's bairns". The author's own family history is a tale of poor, struggling agricultural labourers, coal miners and railway workers striving to achieve more than their working-class existence afforded them. Within his own history are stories of heroism through two world wars, tales of illegitimacy, infant mortality, the poorhouse and grinding poverty. The average reader will be able to relate their family history in the same vein.

Likewise, the genealogy of the Aberdeen heroes of Gothenburg in 1983 reveals a remarkably similar tale of ordinary working-class boys from predominantly poor backgrounds. They achieved something extraordinary. The reader should be aware that it has not been possible to research every aspect of the Dons' ancestors and in the main the detailed research concentrates on their Scottish family history.

The Dons of Gothenburg will remain immortal, even within the confines of this book.

Pride of the Dons.

This is their amazing history.

PRIDE OF THE DONS

**The Gothenburg Greats - Dons players
11 May 1983**

**Nya Ullevi Stadium, Gothenburg,
Sweden**

Chapter 1:

Jim Leighton MBE (Goalkeeper)
Honours as an Aberdeen player:
1 European Cup Winners Cup
1 European Super Cup
2 Scottish Premier League titles
4 Scottish Cups
1 Scottish League Cup

The young Jim Leighton

Named after his paternal grandfather James, Jim Leighton MBE is a Scottish former footballer, who played as a world class goalkeeper. James Leighton was born on 24 July 1958 at the Maternity Hospital, Johnstone, Renfrewshire to his father Samuel Leighton, an engineer fitter, and mother Mary Jane McAvoy. At that time, the Leighton family lived at 26 Ferguslie Walk, Paisley, Renfrewshire. In his youth Leighton played for Eastercraigs Boys Club and then at Dalry Thistle. After leaving school, Leighton worked in the civil service, then joined Aberdeen from Scottish Junior club Dalry

PRIDE OF THE DONS

Thistle in 1977. Before breaking into the Aberdeen first team, he was loaned out by then manager Billy McNeill for one season to Highland League club Deveronvale. He is now inducted into the club's Hall of Fame. On his return to Pittodrie, Leighton found a new manager in charge – the legendary Alex Ferguson. Leighton started his professional career with Aberdeen, where he won seven domestic trophies under Ferguson's management; also, the 1982–83 European Cup Winners' Cup and the 1983 European Super Cup.

Ferguson signed Leighton for Manchester United in 1988, but acrimoniously dropped the goalkeeper after he conceded three goals in the 1990 FA Cup Final. Although it became a crushing disappointment for Leighton, it was seen as a defining watershed moment for Ferguson. Ferguson arguably became the most successful British manager of all time. Leighton also played for Arsenal, Reading, Dundee and Sheffield United, and rebuilt his career after joining Hibernian in 1993. He returned to Aberdeen in 1997, making over 600 league appearances. Leighton played in 91 international matches for Scotland. He was chosen for Scotland's World Cup squads in 1982, 1986, 1990 and 1998, playing in the latter three tournaments.

Jim's parents – Samuel Leighton and Mary Jane McAvoy

A few months after the 1926 General Strike, Jim's father Samuel Leighton was born on 11 November 1926, at 43 Belville Street, Greenock, Renfrewshire, to father James Leighton, an engineer, and his mother Margaret Smith. The birth was registered by his father James Leighton on 12 December 1926 at the Greenock Registry Office. After leaving school Samuel worked as an engineer's fitter. In the same year Adolf Hitler's Nazi Party rose to power in Germany, Jim's mother Mary Jane McAvoy was born on 6 August 1933 at 202 Main Street, Elderslie, to father John McAvoy, a paper maker, and mother Bridget Flynn. The birth was registered by father John McAvoy on 23 August 1933 at the Johnstone Registry Office. After leaving school Mary Jane worked as a carpet factory spool setter.

Samuel Leighton, 30, an engineer's fitter, of 71 Wheatlands Drive, Kilbarchan, Renfrewshire, married Mary Jane McAvoy, 23, a carpet factory spool setter, of 1 Ryefield Place, Johnstone, on 9 February 1957 at St Margaret's RC Church, Johnstone according to Roman Catholic Church. The wedding was conducted by Father Denis J Sheahan, Roman Catholic priest of St Margaret's Church; the best man was J McAvoy, of 1 Ryefield Place, Johnstone, and the bridesmaid was Margaret McAvoy, of 16 Hogg Avenue, Johnstone. Son James Leighton was born on 24 July 1958 at the Maternity Hospital, Johnstone to his father Samuel Leighton, an engineer fitter, and his mother Mary Jane McAvoy. At that time, the Leighton family lived at 26 Ferguslie Walk, Paisley, Renfrewshire.

Jim's paternal grandparents – James Leighton and Margaret Smith

Jim's paternal grandfather James Leighton was born on 20 May 1896 at Milton Terrace, Queen Street, Dunoon, Argyllshire, to father James Leighton, a quarryman, and mother Elizabeth Aitken. The birth was registered by his father James Leighton on 8 June 1896 at the Dunoon Registry Office. However, in 1898, when James was still only 2 years old, his father James died of tuberculosis and his mother took her three sons to live in Kilbarchan, Renfrewshire near her parents' home. In 1901, James, 4, resided at Campbell's Land, Kilbarchan, with his widowed mother Elizabeth Leighton, 29, a dressmaker working at home, brothers Samuel, 9, and Hugh, 7.

After leaving school, James got a job as a message boy in his grandfather's fruit shop. In 1911, James, 14, a fruiterer's message boy, resided at 10 New Street, Kilbarchan, with his widowed grandfather Hugh Aitken, 73, a fruiterer, his widowed mother Elizabeth Leighton, 39, brothers Samuel, 19, an apprentice draughtsman in an engineering works, and Hugh, 17, a law clerk.

DEREK NIVEN

Jim's paternal grandmother Margaret Smith was probably born around 1895 in Renfrewshire to her father Andrew Smith, a grain merchant, and mother Helen Paton. After leaving school, Margaret got a job as a threadmill worker, the main manufacturer locally being the world-renowned Coates of Paisley.

In 1916, during WWI, James Leighton, 19, born in Dunoon, Argyllshire, enlisted in the newly formed Royal Air Force. This is recorded in catalogue AIR 79 at the National Archives, Kew, London. After being demobbed from the RAF, James Leighton, 24, an iron fitter, of 13 Gateside Place, Kilbarchan, married Margaret Smith, 25, a threadmill worker, of 30 Gateside Place, Kilbarchan, on 2 April 1921, at Margaret's home according to the United Free Church. The wedding was conducted by Rev Malcolm Pollock, minister of Kilbarchan United Free; the witnesses were Hugh Aitken Leighton, James's brother, and Elizabeth Smith, Margaret's sister.

Son Samuel Leighton was born on 11 November 1926 at 43 Belville Street, Greenock, Renfrewshire, to his father James Leighton, an engineer, and his mother Margaret Smith. By 1935, James had moved with his family to 7 East William Street, Greenock and during WWII they lived at 58 Belville Street, Greenock. James Leighton, 69, died in 1966 in Johnstone, Renfrewshire and his wife Margaret Leighton nee Smith, 86, died in 1982 in Johnstone.

Jim's maternal grandparents – John McAvoy and Bridget Flynn

The long Victorian era had recently ended when Jim's maternal grandfather John McAvoy or McEvoy was born on 5 July 1901 at 20 Rankin Street, Johnstone, to Irish-born father John McAvoy, a flax mill hand, and mother Elizabeth Murray. In 1911, John, 9, resided at 4 Houston Square, Johnstone, with father John McAvoy, 44, a storeman in a general engineering works, mother Elizabeth, 44, and his other siblings.

Jim's maternal grandmother Bridget Flynn was probably born around 1903 in Renfrewshire to father James Flynn, a foundry labourer, and mother Mary Jane Twigg. John McAvoy, 31, a papermaker, of 4 Church Street, Johnstone, married Bridget Flynn, 29, a tilemaker, of 9 Bridge Street, Linwood, at St Conval's Chapel, Linwood, on 1 October 1932 according to the Roman Catholic Church. The wedding was conducted by Fr Cornelius Donnelly, clergyman at St Conval's; the best man was Charles Flynn, Bridget's brother, and the bridesmaid was Mary McCormack. Daughter Mary Jane McAvoy was born on 6 August 1933 at 202 Main Street, Elderslie to father John McAvoy, a papermaker, and mother Bridget Flynn. Bridget McAvoy nee Flynn, 71, died in 1975 in Johnstone, Renfrewshire and John McAvoy, 83, died in 1985 in Johnstone.

Jim's paternal great-grandparents – James Leighton and Elizabeth Aitken

Jim's paternal great-grandfather also James Leighton was born on 10 March 1860 in Lochwinnoch, Renfrewshire, to father Henry Leighton, a quarryman, and mother Agnes Savage. In 1861, James, 1, resided in High Street, Lochwinnoch with his father Henry Leighton, 41, a vintner, mother Agnes, 24, and his brother William, 5, a scholar. As a boy James was raised in Lochwinnoch, then in Largs, Ayrshire between 1862 and 1865. The family moved to Dunoon, Argyllshire from 1865 until the late 1870s.

His great-grandmother Elizabeth Aitken aka Lizzie was born on 10 April 1871 in Kilbarchan, Renfrewshire to father Hugh Aitken, a railway porter, and mother Susan Rafferty. Around 1890, James and Lizzie, both still single, emigrated to the USA and married on 2 October 1890 in Manhattan, New York City, New York. They then travelled to North Carolina, most likely to Elizabeth City, Pasquotank County. This is where James's sisters Agnes and Alice had settled, both marrying Ownley brothers.

James and Lizzie had 3 known sons; Samuel (b. 8 October 1891, North Carolina), Hugh Aitken (b. ~1894, North Carolina) and James (b. 20 May 1896, Dunoon).

PRIDE OF THE DONS

It appears they could not settle in North Carolina. James and Lizzie returned to Scotland around 1895, settling in Dunoon, where James spent his boyhood. Son James Leighton was born on 20 May 1896 at Milton Terrace, Queen Street, Dunoon to father James Leighton, a quarryman, and mother Elizabeth Aitken.

However, the following year James contracted the dreaded Victorian killer, tuberculosis, at that time, called phthisis. James Leighton, only 34, a quarryman, died on 6 March 1898 at Mill Street, Dunoon of phthisis, after 6 months, as certified by Dr James Moir LRCP. The death was registered by his brother Samuel Leighton on 7 March 1898 at the Dunoon Registry Office. In 1901, Elizabeth Leighton, 29, a widowed dressmaker, moved back to Kilbarchan, residing at Campbell's Land, with sons Samuel, 9, Hugh, 7, and James, 4.

In 1911, Elizabeth Leighton, 39, a widow, resided at 10 New Street, Kilbarchan, with her widowed father Hugh Aitken, 73, a fruiterer, sons Samuel, 19, an apprentice draughtsman in an engineering works, Hugh, 17, a law clerk, and James, 14, a fruiterer's message boy. Elizabeth Leighton nee Aitken, 77, who never remarried, died in 1949 in Kilbarchan.

Jim's paternal great-grandparents – Andrew Smith and Helen Paton

Jim's other paternal great-grandfather Andrew Smith and his great-grandmother Helen Paton were both born around 1870. Andrew Smith, a grain merchant, married Helen Paton and they had 2 known daughters probably born in Renfrewshire; Margaret (b. ~1895) and Elizabeth. Andrew and Helen were still alive in 1921.

Jim's maternal great-grandparents – John McAvoy and Elizabeth Murray

On Jim's maternal line was his great-grandfather John McAvoy (or McEvoy) and his great-grandmother Elizabeth Murray. John McAvoy was born around 1867 in County Down, Ireland and Elizabeth Murray were born around 1867 in Beith, Ayrshire. It is likely that John and Elizabeth cohabited in Ayrshire from around 1891. However, they did not get married until New Year's Day, 1 January 1896 in Kilbirnie, Ayrshire. John and Elizabeth had 8 known children, although, as was common in the Victorian era due to high infant mortality rates, two children died in infancy; in Barrmill, Ayrshire, David (b. ~1894), and in Johnstone, Renfrewshire, Edward (b. ~1897), Mary (b. ~1899), John (b. 5 July 1901), Christina (b. ~1906) and Margaret (b. ~1910).

PRIDE OF THE DONS

Son John was born on 5 July 1901 at 20 Rankin Street, Johnstone to father John McAvoy, a flax mill hand, and mother Elizabeth Murray. On his son's birth certificate, John clearly signed his name 'John McEvoy'. In 1911, John McAvoy, 44, a storeman in a general engineering works, resided at 4 Houston Square, Johnstone, with wife Elizabeth, 44, children David, 17, Edward, 14, both flax mill workers, Mary, 12, John, 9, Christina, 5, all at school, and baby Margaret, 11 months old. Elizabeth McAvoy nee Murray died in 1937 in Johnstone and her husband John McAvoy, 85, a threadmill labourer, died in 1953 in Paisley.

Jim's maternal great-grandparents – James Flynn and Mary Jane Twigg

Jim's other maternal great-grandfather James Flynn and his great-grandmother Mary Jane Twigg were probably born around 1870 and both of Irish descent. James, a foundry labourer, married Mary Jane and they had 2 known children; Bridget (b. ~1903) and Charles. James and Mary Jane were both dead by 1932.

Jim's paternal great-great-grandparents – Henry Lyle Leighton and Agnes Savage

Jim's paternal great-great-grandfather Henry Lyle Leighton (or Lighton), aka Hendry or Harry, was born in Ireland around 1821 and his great-great-grandmother Agnes Savage was born in Largs, Ayrshire around 1837. Henry and his sister Leticia emigrated to Scotland around 1840, working as farm labourers. In 1841, Henry Lighton, 20, an agricultural labourer, and his sister Leticia, 15, a farm servant, resided at Robert Barr's Whitehill Farm in Dalry, Ayrshire. Henry married his first wife and they had a daughter Leticia born in Beith around 1847, although he was soon a widower.

After his wife died, Henry, 30, a labourer, fell on hard times. By 1851 he lived in the St Cuthbert's Charity Workhouse in Edinburgh, although by 1853 he had returned to Ayrshire. Henry Lyle Leighton, a quarryman, married his second wife Agnes Savage on 25 June 1853 in Largs, Ayrshire. They had ten known children; William (b. 2 April 1856, Largs), Henry (b. 2 April 1858, Lochwinnoch, died in infancy), James (b. 10 March 1860, Lochwinnoch), Samuel (b. 2 January 1862, Largs), John (b. 9 August 1864, Largs), Agnes (b. 9 August 1866, Dunoon), Alice Christie (b. 20 June 1868, Dunoon), son Henry (b. 3 February 1871, Dunoon), Margaret Livingston Christie (b. 18 February 1873, Dunoon) and Jessie (b. 29 December 1880, Greenock West). In 1861, Henry Leighton, 41, a vintner, resided in High Street, Lochwinnoch with wife Agnes, 24, sons William, 5, a scholar,

James, 1, and Alice Savage, 18, a domestic servant and Agnes's younger sister. The wine business failed to flourish and by 1871, Henry Leighton, 45, a stone breaker, resided at St Mungo Terrace, Edward Street, Dunoon, with wife Agnes, 34, a stone breaker's wife, children Leticia, 24, Samuel, 9, Agnes, 5, Alice Christie, 3, and also Henry, 3 months old. Henry Leighton, 58, died in 1886 in the Kelvin district of Glasgow and his wife Agnes was dead by 1898.

Daughters Agnes and Alice emigrated to the USA and both married into the Ownley family. In 1910, Alice, 35, and husband Hubert Ownley, 23, a baker for the Box Lunch Company, resided in Cincinnati, Ohio with their family. In 1920, Agnes, 55, resided in Mount Hermon, North Carolina, with husband Tim Ownley, 65, a farmer, and their family. Alice Leighton Ownley, 68, the wife of Hubert Eley Ownley, died on 7 May 1944, during WW2, in Elizabeth City, Pasquotank, NC. Agnes Leighton Ownley, 93, wife of Timothy Stewart Ownley, died on 21 February 1960 in Mount Hermon, Pasquotank, NC.

Jim's other paternal great-great-grandparents – Hugh Aitken and Susan Rafferty

Jim's other paternal line great-great-grandfather Hugh Aitken was born around 1838 in Kilbarchan, Renfrewshire and as a boy of 13, Hugh worked as a woollen hand loom weaver. His great-great-grandmother Susan Rafferty was born around 1847 in East Kilbride, Lanarkshire. Hugh Aitken, a railway porter, married Susan Rafferty and they had 2 known children; Alexander (b. ~1865, Bridge of Weir) and Elizabeth (b. 10 April 1871, Kilbarchan).

In 1871, Hugh Aitken, 30, a railway porter with the Glasgow & South Western Railway, resided at Laird's Land, Kilbarchan, with pregnant wife Susan, 24, a railway porter's wife, and son Alexander, 6. Hugh's wife Susan, 34, died in 1881 and Hugh never remarried. In 1911, Hugh Aitken, 73, a widowed fruiterer, resided at 10 New Street, Kilbarchan, with daughter Elizabeth Leighton, 39, a widow, his 3 grandsons Samuel, 19, an apprentice draughtsman in an engineering works, Hugh, 17, a law clerk, and James, 14, a fruiterer's message boy, obviously working in his grandfather's fruit shop. Hugh Aitken died in 1912 as registered in Airdrie, Lanarkshire.

Chapter 2:

Doug Rougvie (right back)
Honours as an Aberdeen player:
1 European Cup Winners Cup
1 European Super Cup
2 Scottish League titles
3 Scottish Cups

The young Doug Rougvie

Douglas Rougvie aka Doug was born on 24 May 1956 at 82 Navitie Park, Ballingry, Fife, to father Gordon James Rougvie, a coal miner shot-firer, and mother Margaret Hodge. Rougvie is a Scottish former footballer, who played mainly for Aberdeen and Chelsea. A hard-tackling and committed defender, Rougvie, who was signed by manager Jimmy Bonthrone, played for Aberdeen between 1975 and 1984, arguably the most successful period in the club's history. After debuting for Aberdeen in an away friendly against Persepolis of Iran in the summer of 1974, he made 279 appearances and scored 21 goals.

DEREK NIVEN

He won the Scottish League championship in 1979–80 and 1983–84, the Scottish Cup in 1982, 1983 and 1984, the European Cup Winners' Cup and European Super Cup, both in 1983. Rougvie was the first player sent off in a Scottish League Cup final in 1979. While an Aberdeen player, Rougvie played one international game for Scotland in 1983. He signed for newly promoted Chelsea in 1984 for £150,000. In 1987 he transferred to Brighton and Hove Albion and had short spells with Shrewsbury Town, Fulham, Dunfermline Athletic and Montrose.

Doug's parents – Gordon James Rougvie and Margaret Hodge

Doug's father Gordon James Rougvie was born on 14 March 1925 at Novar Cottage, Dundonald, Cardenden, Auchterderran, Fife to father James Rougvie, a coal miner, and mother Amelia Annie Goodsell. The birth was registered by father James Rougvie on 1 April 1925 at the Auchterderran Registry Office. His mother Margaret Hodge was born on 19 May 1924 at 297 Main Street, Bellshill to father Adam Bunyan Hodge, a coal miner, and mother Margaret Barr. The birth was registered by father Adam Hodge on 7 June 1924 at the Bellshill Registry Office.

PRIDE OF THE DONS

Main Street, Bellshill has several other Scottish football historical connections. Billy McNeill, captain of the Lisbon Lions, was born in his Lithuanian grandparents', Kazis and Urzula, miner's cottage at 116 Main Street. Alfred Gemmell, the father of Tommy Gemmell, another Lisbon Lion, was born at 348 Main Street.

Sir Matt Busby, manager of Manchester United, born in Old Orbiston, Bellshill, has four relatives all commemorated on the Bellshill War Memorial in front of Bellshill Academy on Main Street; his father Alexander Busby, uncles William and Thomas Greer and uncle William Mathie.

Gordon James Rougvie, 23, a coal miner, of 31 Kirkland Avenue, Lochore in Fife, married his wife Margaret Hodge, 24, a bus conductress, of 47 South Glencraig, Lochgelly, on 6 August 1948 in a civil ceremony at the registrar's office in Lochgelly. The wedding was conducted by Edward Herron, assistant registrar; the best man was Samuel Dalton and the bridesmaid was Winifred A Rougvie, Gordon's sister. Gordon and Margaret's son Douglas Rougvie was born on 24 May 1956 at 82 Navitie Park, Ballingry, Fife. Father Gordon Rougvie registered the birth on 28 May 1956 at the Glencraig Registry Office.

Doug's paternal grandparents – James Rougvie and Amelia Annie Goodsell

Doug's paternal grandfather James Rougvie was born on 14 May 1892 in the coal-mining village of Thornton, Markinch, Fife to father James Rougvie, a coal miner, and mother Agnes Stoddart Barclay. In 1911, James, 19, a waggon builder, resided at Main Street, Thornton, Markinch, with his father James Rougvie, 53, a coal miner hewer, mother Agnes, 47, and his other siblings. At that time Thornton had a huge railway freight marshalling yard. At the outbreak of WWI, James enlisted as Private S/8931 in the Royal Highlanders. He entered the French theatre of war on 31 October 1915. James fought and survived the horrors of the Western Front until Armistice Day on 11 November 1918. James was awarded the Victory Medal, the British War Medal and the 1915 Star. He was demobbed and transferred to Class Z reservist on 20 January 1919.

Doug's paternal grandmother Amelia Annie Goodsell was born in 2nd Quarter 1893 in Salehurst, Sussex to father William Goodsell, a farm labourer, and mother Annie Maria Collins (Ticehurst, 2a/115). In 1901, Amelia A, 8, resided at Wellington Road, East Ham in Essex, with her widowed mother Annie M Goodsell, 46, a shirt machinist, her sisters Mabel Ivy, 10, Hilda G, 7, and Ada Louise, 5. Back in civvies, James Rougvie married Amelia Annie Goodsell on 25 November 1920 in London as registered in the 4th Quarter (Hendon, Middlesex 3A/93).

James and Amelia moved to the Auchterderran coalfields in Fife, which must have been a real shock for Amelia after growing up in rural Sussex. Son Gordon James Rougvie was born on 14 March 1925 at Novar Cottage, Dundonald, Cardenden, Auchterderran, Fife to father James Rougvie, a coal miner, and mother Amelia Annie Goodsell. In 1930, the Rougvie family lived at Belmont Cottage, Cluny Road, Auchterderran, where they remained during WWII. James Rougvie, 70, a coal miner, died in 1959 in Lochore, Fife. His wife Amelia Annie Rougvie nee Goodsell, 91, died in 1984 also in Lochore.

Doug's maternal grandparents – Adam Bunyan Hodge and Margaret Barr

Doug's maternal grandfather Adam Bunyan Hodge was born on 10 April 1890 in Coylton Row, Coylton, Ayrshire to father John Hodge, a coal miner, and mother Elizabeth Bunyan. Doug's maternal grandmother Margaret Barr was probably born around 1885 in Lanarkshire to father John Barr, an estate forester, and mother Mary Gallagher.

Adam Hodge, 22, a coal miner, of 31 George Street, Bellshill, married Margaret Barr, 27, of 16 Craig Place, Bellshill, on 31 May 1912 at the Manse, Bellshill, according to the Church of Scotland. The wedding was conducted by Rev Gavin Warnock DD, minister of Bellshill; the best man was Joseph Barr, Margaret's brother, and the bridesmaid was Matilda Ritchie.

At the outbreak of WWI, Adam, as a coal miner, was deemed in 'protected employment' and he never served in the military during the war. Adam and wife Margaret had five known children in Bellshill. Son Matthew Barr Hodge was born on 9 January 1913 at 16 Craig Place, Bellshill. Son Adam Hodge was born on 22 March 1915 at The Kennels, Carnbroe, Bellshill. Daughter Elizabeth Hodge was born on 21 February 1918 at 297 Main Street, Bellshill. Son John Hodge was born on 9 May 1919 at 18 Craig Place, Bellshill. Finally, daughter Margaret Hodge was born on 19 May 1924 at 297 Main Street, Bellshill. Margaret Hodge nee Barr, only 53, died in 1937 in Lochgelly, Fife. Her husband Adam Hodge, only 50, a coal miner died in 1940, during WWII, also in Lochgelly.

Doug's paternal great-grandparents – James Rougvie and Agnes Stoddart Barclay

Doug's paternal great-grandfather James Rougvie was born around 1857 in Fordell (or Dalgetty), Fife to father William Rougvie, a coal miner, and mother Margaret Baillie. Great-grandmother Agnes Stoddart Barclay was born around 1864 in Dysart, Fife to father James Barclay, a railway servant, and mother Helen

Maule. James Rougvie, 21, a coalminer, married his first wife Alison Farquhar, 17, a carpet factory hand, both of the Common, Newbattle, Stobhill, Midlothian, on 27 May 1878 at the Common according to the Free Church of Scotland. The wedding was conducted by the Rev A Gillon Macalpine, minister of the Free Church; the witnesses were George and William Rougvie, James's brothers. James and Alison had two known sons in Lasswade; William (b. ~1879) and Joseph (b. ~1881). In 1881, James Rougvie, 22, a coal miner, resided at the Common, Newbattle, Stobhill with wife Alison, 20, sons William, 2, and Joseph, 4 months old, next door to his parents William and Margaret. Tragically, Alison was dead by 1888 and James returned to the Fife coalfields.

James Rougvie, 30, a widowed coal miner, married his second wife Agnes Stoddart Barclay, 24, a domestic servant, both of Thornton, Markinch on 23 March 1888 in Thornton according to the Church of Scotland. The wedding was conducted by the Rev D Macfarlane Wilson, minister of Thornton; the best man was William Robertson and the bridesmaid was Nellie M Barclay, Agnes's sister. James and Agnes had 13 known children born in Thornton, Markinch, although one died in infancy; Alexander (b. ~1890), David (b. ~1891), James (b. 14 May 1892), Helen aka Nellie (b. ~1893), Walter (b. ~1894), Minnie (b. ~1897), John (b. ~1898), Agnes (b. ~1900), Sarah (b. ~1902), Charles (b. ~1904), Elizabeth aka Lizzie (b. ~1909) and Ralph (b. ~1910). Son James Rougvie was born on 14 May 1892 in the coal-mining village of Thornton, Markinch, Fife to father James

Rougvie, a coal miner, and his mother Agnes Stoddart Barclay.

In 1911, James Rougvie, 53, a coal miner hewer, resided at Main Street, Thornton, Markinch, with wife Agnes, 47, children Alexander, 21, David, 20, both coal miner hewers, James, 19, a waggon builder, Nellie, 18, a thread turner in a cotton spinning factory, Walter, 17, a coal miner drawer, Minnie, 14, a domestic servant, then, at school, Agnes, 11, Sarah, 9, Charles, 7, and infants Lizzie, 2, and Ralph, 9 months old. James Rougvie, 71, died in 1929 in Thornton and his wife Agnes Rougvie nee Barclay, 84, died in 1948 also in Thornton.

Doug's other paternal great-grandparents – William Goodsell and Annie Maria Collins

Doug's other paternal great-grandfather William Goodsell was born around 1871 and christened on 27 August 1871 in Salehurst, Sussex to father William Goodsell and mother Frances Austing Hicks. In 1879, William's father died aged 41. In 1881, William, 9, a scholar, resided in Salehurst, with his mother Frances Goodsell, 40, a widowed innkeeper, and his siblings. His great-grandmother Annie Maria Collins was born around 1858 in Hoxton, London. William Goodsell, a farm labourer, married heavily pregnant Annie Maria Collins in the 1st Quarter 1891 (Ticehurst, Sussex 2B/165).

PRIDE OF THE DONS

William and Annie had 4 daughters; Mabel Ivy (b. ~1891, Salehurst), Amelia Annie (b. 1893, Salehurst), Hilda Gertrude, (b. ~1894, West Ham) and Ada Louise, (b. ~1896, West Ham). In 1891, William Goodsell, 22, a farm labourer and licensed victualler, resided at Church Lane, Old Eight Bells, Salehurst, with Annie M, 33, daughter Mabel Ivy, 1 month old, and 3 nieces, probably orphaned, Lucy L O'Hea, 15, Eveline F A Collins, 12, and Minnie M Collins, 3.

William Goodsell, only 29, a farm labourer, died in 1st Quarter 1898 in West Ham, London, leaving Annie to raise 4 young daughters. In 1901, Annie M Goodsell, 46, a shirt machinist, resided at Wellington Road, East Ham, Essex, with daughters Mabel Ivy, 10, Amelia A, 8, Hilda G, 7, and Ada Louise, 5. Annie never remarried and lived a long life, living through both World Wars. Annie Maria Goodsell nee Collins, 91, died in 1st Quarter 1947 (Hendon, Middlesex 5F/155).

Doug's maternal great-grandparents – John Hodge and Elizabeth Bunyan

Doug's maternal great-grandfather John Hodge and great-grandmother Elizabeth Bunyan were born around 1870 probably in Ayrshire. John Hodge, a coal miner, married Elizabeth Bunyan on 23 September 1886 in Coylton, Ayrshire. It is likely they had a very large family, with two known sons identified. Son Adam Bunyan Hodge was born on 10 April 1890 in Coylton Row, Coylton, Ayrshire to father John Hodge, a coal miner, and mother Elizabeth Bunyan. Son Francis Bunyan Hodge was born on 13 January 1914 at 74 Muirpark Rows, Bellshill, Lanarkshire, to father John Hodge, a coal miner, and mother Elizabeth Bunyan. Elizabeth Hodge nee Bunyan, 57, died in 1928 in Bellshill.

Doug's maternal great-grandparents – John Barr and Mary Gallagher

Doug's other maternal great-grandfather John Barr and great-grandmother Mary Gallagher were born around 1860 probably in Lanarkshire. John Barr, an estate forester, married Mary Gallagher and they had 2 known children; son Joseph and daughter Margaret born around 1885 in Lanarkshire. John and Mary were still alive in 1912 in Bellshill, Lanarkshire.

Doug's paternal great-great-grandparents – William Rougvie and Margaret Baillie

Doug's great-great-grandfather William Rougvie was born around 1820 in Kinghorn, Fife and his great-great-grandmother Margaret Baillie was born around 1823 in Kirkcaldy, Fife. William Rougvie, a flax dresser, married Margaret Baillie around 1843 and they had five known sons; in Kinghorn, William (b. ~1844), Alexander (b. ~1847), Charles (b. ~1850); in Dalgetty, James (b. ~1857) and John (b. ~1863). In 1851, William Rougvie, 31, a flax dresser, resided at South Street, Scoonie, Fife with wife Margaret, 27, sons William, 7, a scholar, Alexander, 3, and Charles, 8 months old.

By the early 1880s, William had moved from the Fife coalmines to those across the Forth in Midlothian. In 1881, William Rougvie, 61, a coal miner, resided at the Common, Newbattle, Stobhill, Midlothian, with wife Margaret, 58, son John, 18, a coal miner, grandsons William, 4, and George Reid, 2. Living next door was son James Rougvie, 22, a coal miner, daughter-in-law Alison, 20, grandsons William, 2, and Joseph, 4 months old. William Rougvie, 68, died in 1888 in Markinch, Fife. His wife Margaret Rougvie nee Baillie, 83, died in 1907 in Kinghorn, Fife.

Doug's paternal great-great-grandparents – William Goodsell and Frances Austing Hicks

Doug's other paternal great-great-grandfather William Goodsell was born around 1838 in Ewhurst, Sussex. His great-great-grandmother Frances Austing Hicks was probably born illegitimately around 1842 in

DEREK NIVEN

Etchingham, Sussex to father William Cheesman and mother Hannah Hicks.

William Goodsell, a licensed victualler, married Frances Austing Hicks in 1st Quarter 1865 (Ticehurst 2B/126) and they had 6 known children in Salehurst; Alice (b. ~1862, possibly illegitimate), Frances (b. ~1867, died in infancy), Kate (b. ~1869, died in infancy), sons William (b. ~1871), Fred (b. ~1874) and Arthur (b. ~1877). In 1871, William Goodsell, 32, a licensed victualler, resided at the Seven Stars Inn, Robertsbridge, Salehurst, with his wife Frances, 29, daughters Alice, 8, a scholar, Frances, 4, a scholar, Kate, 2, and young Ann Weller, 17, a domestic servant.

William Goodsell, 41, an innkeeper at Robertsbridge, Salehurst, Sussex, died in 1879. He was buried on 5 March 1879 in St Mary's Churchyard, Salehurst by Rev R W Looseman, vicar of St Mary's. After William died Frances continued to run the Seven Stars Inn. In 1881, Frances Goodsell, 40, a widowed innkeeper, resided in Salehurst, with children Alice, 19, an innkeeper's assistant, William, 9, Fred, 7, both scholars, and Arthur, 4. In 1891, Frances Goodsell, 49, a widow living on her own means, resided at Swiftsden Farm, Etchingham, with her father William Cheesman, 80, a retired farmer living on his own means, mother Hannah, 69, and their granddaughter Kate Patey, 17. Frances Goodsell nee Hicks, 65, died in 1st Quarter 1905 (Eastbourne, Sussex 2B/69).

Chapter 3:

**John McMaster (left back)
Honours as an Aberdeen player:
1 European Cup Winners Cup
2 Scottish League titles
3 Scottish Cups**

The young John McMaster

John McMaster was born on 23 February 1955 at 4 Chalmers Street, Greenock, Renfrewshire to father John McMaster, a riveter, and mother Susan Dixon. The birth was registered by his father John McMaster on 11 March 1955 at the Greenock Registry Office. John was raised in Greenock and grew up a Greenock Morton fan. He was a Scottish former professional footballer who played the bulk of his career with Aberdeen. He joined the Dons from Port Glasgow Juniors in 1972 under their then manager Jimmy Bonthrone.

McMaster made 316 appearances (47 as a substitute) and scored 20 goals for Aberdeen. He secured multiple winners' medals between 1974 and 1986, including the famous European Cup Winners' Cup in 1983, two Scottish League titles and three Scottish Cups.

McMaster received the kiss of life during a Scottish League Cup game against Rangers on 3 September 1980, after Willie Johnston stamped on his neck at Ibrox Stadium. He was also badly injured against Liverpool in the European Cup a month later, keeping him out for a year. In 1987, he signed for his hometown club Morton, before retiring to become assistant manager of the club. During this time, he developed several players including future Aberdeen manager Derek McInnes. He has since worked as a scout for Swansea City in the west of Scotland. In November 2017, McMaster was one of four inductees into the Aberdeen Hall of Fame.

John's parents – John McMaster and Susan Dixon

John's father John McMaster was born on 11 March 1920 at 15 Main Street, Greenock, Renfrewshire, to father William McMaster, a riveter journeyman, and mother Mary Richmond. The birth was registered by his father William McMaster on 17 March 1920 at Greenock Registry Office.

PRIDE OF THE DONS

John's mother Susan Dixon was born on 27 November 1922 in Greenock to father William Dixon, a railwayman, and mother Bridget Canning. John McMaster, 23, a riveter journeyman in the Clyde shipyards at Greenock, of 14 Leitch Street, Greenock, married wife Susan Dixon, 20, a bus conductress, of 2 Chalmers Street, Greenock, on 10 September 1943, during WWII, at Crawfurdsburn Church, Greenock according to the Church of Scotland. The wedding was conducted by Rev John Graham, minister of Crawfurdsburn; the two witnesses were Janet Roddick and William Patterson.

John and Susan's son John was born on 23 February 1955 at 4 Chalmers Street, Greenock. The birth was registered by John's father John McMaster on 11 March 1955 at the Greenock Registry Office. They also had a son Andrew McMaster. John McMaster was dead before 1986, the year his wife Susan had died of cancer. Susan McMaster nee Dixon, 63, the widow of John McMaster, a riveter, died on 23 August 1986 at 2 Cedar Crescent, Greenock of bronchial carcinoma as certified by Dr G Eric Gowling. The death was registered by her son Andrew McMaster, of 12 Bell Street, Greenock, on 25 August 1986 at the Greenock Registry Office. Susan had lived to see her son John win the European Cup Winner's Cup.

John's paternal grandparents – William McMaster and Mary Richmond

John's paternal grandfather William McMaster was born around 1876 in Greenock to Irish-born parents John McMaster, a labourer, and Mary Boyd. In 1881, William, 5, resided at 7 Main Street, Cartsburn, Greenock, with father John McMaster, 46, a sawmill labourer, mother Mary, 44, and his other siblings.

John's grandmother Mary Richmond was born around 1877 probably in Glasgow to father Andrew Richmond and mother Jean Munn. William McMaster, 27, an apprentice riveter, of 9 Main Street, Greenock, married Mary Richmond or Murray, 26, a widow, of 11 Main Street, Greenock, on 19 June 1903 according to the Church of Scotland. The wedding was conducted by Rev John Graham, minister of Greenock East Parish; the best man was John McMaster, William's brother, and the bridesmaid was Janet Richmond, Mary's sister. Mary had previously been married to her first husband surnamed Murray but was a widow by 1903.

Son John McMaster was born on 11 March 1920 at 15 Main Street, Greenock, Renfrewshire, to father William McMaster, a riveter journeyman, and mother Mary Richmond. The birth was registered by his father William McMaster on 17 March 1920 at the Greenock Registry Office. William and Mary were still alive in Greenock in 1943, during WWII. William McMaster, 74, died in 1950 in Greenock.

John's maternal grandparents – William Dixon and Bridget Canning

John's maternal grandfather William Dixon was born around 1892 in Greenock to father John Dixon, a farm labourer, and mother Bridget Gillespie.

John's maternal grandmother Bridget Canning was born around 1895. William Dixon, a labourer on the Glasgow & South Western Railway, married Bridget Canning and they had a daughter Susan (b. 27 November 1922) in Greenock. In 1923, William was transferred to the London Midland & Scottish Railway Company during the amalgamation of the "Big Four".

Three days before the infamous Clydebank Blitz, during WWII, William Dixon, only 49, a railway labourer with the London Midland & Scottish Railway Coy, of 2 Chalmers Street, Greenock, died on 10 March 1941 in the Greenock Royal Infirmary of a compound fracture of both legs, which occurred the previous day, as certified by Dr A M King MB.

The death was registered by C Canning, who was William Dixon's brother-in-law, of 3 Ladyburn Building, Greenock, on 12 March 1941 at the Greenock Registry Office. In a Register of Corrected Entries in Volume 23 at Page 59, it was recorded that William Dixon, 49, died on 10 March 1941 of a *'compound fracture of both legs, surgical shock. Injuries sustained through being run over during shunting operations in the course of his employment per finding of Sheriff.'* This was certified by Procurator Fiscal L T C MacLachlan on 25 April 1941 at Greenock. William's wife Bridget Dixon nee Canning was still alive in 1943, but died in 1982 in Greenock.

John's paternal great-grandparents – John McMaster and Mary Boyd

John's paternal great-grandfather John McMaster was born around 1835, probably in Ballymena, County Antrim, Ulster Province, Ireland, to his father William McMaster, a handloom weaver, and mother Jane Campbell. John's great-grandmother Mary Boyd was born around 1836, probably in Ballymena in Co. Antrim, Ulster, to father Hugh Boyd, a labourer, and mother Margaret Smillie. A year after the end of the devastating Irish Potato Famine, John McMaster married Mary Boyd on 4 April 1853, in Ballymena, County Antrim. John and wife Mary had six known children; in Ballymena, Hugh (b. ~1857), in Greenock, Jane (b. ~1863), John (b. ~1869), Thomas (b. ~1871), Mary (b. ~1874) and William (b. ~1876).

John came to Scotland around 1860 seeking employment and in 1861, John McMaster, aged around 30, a sugarhouse labourer, lodged in Market Street, Greenock. Raw sugar was imported from the Caribbean colonies and sugar refining was a major industry in Greenock at that time. This spawned large firms such as Tate & Lyle. Son William McMaster was born around 1876 in Greenock to father John McMaster, a labourer, and mother Mary Boyd. In 1881, John McMaster, 46, now a sawmill labourer, resided at 7 Main Street, Cartsburn, Greenock, with his wife Mary, 44, children Hugh, 24, a brass finisher, Jane, 18, a pottery worker, John, 12, Thomas, 10, Mary, 7, all scholars, and William, 5.

Mary McMaster nee Boyd, only 55, died on 15 September 1887 at 7 Main Street, Greenock of malignant liver disease for 5 months and jaundice, as certified by Dr John Macdougall MD. The death was registered by her widowed husband John McMaster, a labourer, on 16 September 1887 at the Greenock Registry Office.

In 1901, John McMaster, 64, a general labourer, resided at 9 Main Street, Greenock, with daughter Mary, 26, a felt worker, and son William, 24, an apprentice ship riveter. Also boarding at John's home were Mary Mitchell, 21, a pottery worker, and John's grandsons Bernard Rafferty, 3, William Rafferty, 2, and John Rafferty, 4 months old. John McMaster, 65, a labourer, died on 2 January 1906 at 9 Main Street, Greenock of epithelioma of the lips and exhaustion as certified by Dr William Walker LRCP&S Edinburgh. The death was registered by his son Hugh McMaster, of 4 Hay Street, Greenock, on 3 January 1906 at the Greenock Registry Office.

John's paternal great-grandparents – Andrew Richmond and Jean Munn

John's other paternal great-grandfather Andrew Richmond and great-grandmother Jean Munn were born around 1850, possibly in Glasgow, Lanarkshire. Andrew Richmond married Jean Munn on 2 July 1874 in Glasgow and they had 2 known daughters; Mary (b. ~1877) and Janet. Andrew Richmond was dead by 1903, but his wife Jean was still alive by then.

John's maternal great-grandparents – John Dixon and Bridget Gillespie

John's maternal great-grandfather John Dixon and great-grandmother Bridget Gillespie were born around 1865. John Dixon, a farm labourer, married Bridget Gillespie and had a son William (b. ~1892). John Dixon, a farm labourer, was dead by 1941, but his wife Bridget was still alive by then.

John's paternal great-great-grandparents – William McMaster and Jane Campbell

John's paternal great-great-grandfather William McMaster and great-great-grandmother Jane Campbell were born around 1810 in Ireland, probably in County Antrim, Ulster Province. William McMaster, a hand loom weaver, married Jane Campbell and had a son John (b. ~1835) in County Antrim. William McMaster was still alive in 1853.

John's paternal great-great-grandparents – Hugh Boyd and Margaret Smillie

John's other paternal great-great-grandfather Hugh Boyd and great-great-grandmother Margaret Smillie were born around 1810 in Ireland. Hugh Boyd, a labourer, married Margaret Smillie and had a daughter Mary (b. ~1836) in Ireland. Hugh, a labourer, and his wife Margaret were both dead by 1887.

Chapter 4:

Neale Cooper (right half)
Honours as an Aberdeen player:
1 European Cup Winners Cup
1 European Super Cup
2 Scottish League titles
4 Scottish Cups
1 Scottish League Cup

The young Neale Cooper

Neale James Cooper was born on 24 November 1963 at the Dooars and Darjeeling Nursing Home, Darjeeling, West Bengal, India, to father Douglas Quin Cooper, a tea planter, and mother Anne Paterson Clark. The Cooper family lived in one of the 'burra sahib' bungalows and Douglas worked in management at Dam Dim Tea Estate, Jalpaiguri, West Bengal. The family had returned to Aberdeen as his father had heart problems, and the young Neale was only six years old when his father died.

Cooper is a former Scottish football player, coach and manager. He attended Airyhall Primary School and Hazlehead Academy in Aberdeen. After a youth spell with King Street during 1978–79, he began his senior career with Aberdeen in 1979, the team he had supported as a boy. Initially, he moved into a flat in Aberdeen, but Alex Ferguson sent him back to live with his widowed mother to curb his wild, youthful tendencies.

He played as a midfielder during the 1980s and 1990s, most prominently for Alex Ferguson's Aberdeen team. A first-team regular from the start of 1981–82 season, he starred in midfield for the Dons for five seasons. He won two Scottish League championships, four Scottish Cups, one League Cup, the 1983 European Cup Winners' Cup and the European Super Cup. Cooper later played for Aston Villa, Rangers, Reading, followed by Dunfermline Athletic and Ross County. Cooper then became a coach, and managed English sides Hartlepool United (twice) and Gillingham, and in Scotland with Ross County and Peterhead.

Neale's parents – Douglas Quin Cooper and Anne Paterson Clark

Neale's father Douglas Quin Cooper was born on 27 November 1928 at 12 Howburn Place, St Machar, Aberdeen, to father William John Cooper, a commercial traveller, and mother Emmeline Frances Quin. The birth was registered by his father W J Cooper on 17 December 1928 at the Aberdeen Registry Office. Neale's mother Anne Paterson Clark was born on 7 August 1927 at 70 Forest Avenue, St Machar, Aberdeen, to her father James Paterson Clark, a commercial traveller, and her mother Annie Black Cameron. The birth was registered by her father James P Clark on 27 August 1927 at the Aberdeen Registry Office.

Douglas Q Cooper, 21, emigrated to Darjeeling, India to work as a tea garden assistant. He sailed on 20 May 1950, departing from Liverpool on board the Anchor Line's *S.S. Cilicia*, bound for Bombay (now Mumbai). Having returned to Aberdeen for a spell, he later sailed again to work as a tea planter on 10 December 1954. He left from Southampton on board the P&O Line's *S.S. Canton*, once again bound for Bombay. Douglas Quin Cooper married Anne Paterson Clark around this time. He made a further sailing, aged 29, and married to Anne, on 18 December 1957, departing from the port of Southampton on board the P&O Line's *S.S. Chusan*, again bound for Bombay. Anne Paterson Cooper sailed alongside her husband.

Douglas and Anne's son Neale James Cooper was born on 24 November 1963 at Dooars & Darjeeling Nursing Home, Darjeeling in West Bengal. Neale's mother Anne Paterson Cooper registered the birth by application, received on 17 February 1964 at the British High Commissioners Office in Calcutta (now Kolkata).

PRIDE OF THE DONS

At that time Douglas worked as a tea planter at Dam Dim Tea Estate in Jalpaiguri, West Bengal. Dam Dim Tea Estate is spread over 1,500 hectares with 738 hectares of planted tea. The estate is divided into three divisions namely Hatkhola, Barrons and the North Grant Division. Hatkhola, meaning 'open market', was the first division planted in the late 19th century. The tea factory was also set up there and the estate was known as Hatkhola Tea Estate. The company applied for and successfully received permission to cultivate tea in the area towards the south. The division was named 'Barrons' in honour of the official who granted permission. In keeping with the same tradition, the North Grant Division was named after Mr. North, the District Commissioner of Jalpaiguri at the time of planting the division. In the intermittent period, the Hatkhola factory was gutted in a fire and a factory was rebuilt in Barrons Division.

The estate name was changed to Dam Dim. The name Dam Dim has its origins in the name of an insect – Dim Dima, found in North East India. A recently retired senior executive and colleague of Douglas Cooper at Dam Dim remembered, *"Mr. Cooper to be a smart and handsome gentleman, who was pretty lively in the social circles. He was also very well considered for his management skills."* Douglas Quin Cooper, only 40, died on 6 October 1969 at 47 North Deeside Road, Beildside, Peterculter, Aberdeenshire of a myocardial infarction and atherosclerotic heart disease as certified by Dr G Shirriffs MB ChB. The death was registered by his widow Anne P Cooper on 6 October 1969 at Peterculter Registry Office.

Neale's paternal grandparents – William John Cooper and Emmeline Frances Quin

Neale's paternal grandfather was William John Cooper born on 10 March 1897 at 60 Broomhill Road, Old Machar, Aberdeen to his father George Cooper, an upholsterer, and mother Emma Crory Black. In 1911, William J, 14, resided at 250 Union Grove, Holburn in Aberdeen, with his father George Cooper, 48, an upholsterer, mother Emma, 40, and his other siblings. Neale's paternal grandmother Emmeline Frances Quin was born in 1899 in Penicuik, Midlothian to father John Quin, a commercial traveller, and mother Emmeline Holland.

William John Cooper, 26, a commercial traveller, of 50 Union Grove, St Machar, Aberdeen, married Emmeline Frances Quin, 24, of Viewbank, Penicuik, Midlothian, on 26 October 1923 at 17 Union Terrace in a civil ceremony by warrant of the Sheriff Substitute of Aberdeen, Kincardine and Banff. The witnesses were John Quin, Emmeline's brother, and Margaret Emslie or Quin, Emmeline's sister-in-law. Son Douglas Quin Cooper was born on 27 November 1928 at 12 Howburn Place, St Machar, Aberdeen, to his father William John Cooper, a commercial traveller, and mother Emmeline Frances Quin. William John Cooper, 43, died in 1940, during WWII, in Haymarket, Edinburgh. Emmeline Frances Cooper nee Quin was dead before 1969.

Neale's maternal grandparents – James Paterson Clark and Annie Black Cameron

Neale's maternal grandfather James Paterson Clark was born on 10 December 1896 at 330 Saracen Street, Possilpark, Glasgow to father Adam Clark, a patternmaker journeyman, and mother Agnes Paterson. The birth was registered by his father Adam Clark on 28 December 1898 at the Maryhill Registry Office. In 1911, James P, 14, an office boy in a ship's brokerage, resided at 215 Saracen Street, Possilpark, Glasgow, with his father Adam Clark, 49, an instrument maker's patternmaker, mother Agnes, 46, and his other siblings. Neale's maternal grandmother Annie Black Cameron was born on 13 September 1894 in Glasgow to father William Cameron, a schoolmaster, and mother Susan Black. She was baptized in St Enoch's Free Church of Scotland on Waterloo Street, Glasgow.

At the outbreak of WWI in August 1914, James Paterson Clark enlisted as Private 6841 in the 5th Battalion Scottish Rifles, the Cameronians. He was renumbered as Private 200558 in the 1/5th Scottish Rifles, based at Maryhill Barracks in Glasgow. James' battalion landed in Le Havre, France to join the British Expeditionary Force on 5 November 1914. It was assigned to fight on the hard-pressed River Aisne.

The Cameronians participated in the famous Christmas Day truce of 1914, when a British team played a German team at football. James would have seen some action at the dreadful battles of the Somme in 1916, the Arras Offensive and 3rd Ypres in 1917, the Lys, on the Hindenburg Line and the Final Advance on Picardy in 1918. He was commissioned as a 2nd Lieutenant on 14 May 1917 and having survived all the horrors of the Western Front, he was awarded the 1914 Star, British War and Victory Medals.

James Paterson Clark, 27, a commercial traveller, of 138 Saracen Street, Possilpark, Glasgow, married Annie Black Cameron, 30, a typist, of 76 Mossgiel Road, Newlands, Glasgow, on 6 September 1924 at the posh Marlborough House, Langside Avenue, Glasgow according to the United Free Church of Scotland. The wedding was conducted by Rev Robert Wilson, minister of South Shawlands UF Church; the best man was James Crawford Laing and the bridesmaid was Sarah McGregor Cameron, Annie's sister. The author and his wife were members of South Shawlands Church in the 1980s.

Marlborough House, at Shawlands Cross, was for many years one of Glasgow's premier venues for weddings, dances, bridge and whist drives and society meetings. It was designed by Whyte & Nichol in Edwardian Baroque style and built for J H Hamilton and W J Smith Partners. The Marlborough's plush suites were named after the Duke of Marlborough's early 18th century battles; Oudenarde, Malplaquet, Ramillies and

Blenheim. During the 1950s the venue became a hub for the music and youth revolution represented by the arrival of Rock and Roll. Billy Connolly performed there in the 3 City String Band, in the early Seventies, for the princely sum of £75; the following year he sold out the Glasgow Apollo. In the mid-1970s, before licensing laws were relaxed, the author met his cousin Jim Lynch on a Sunday at The Marlborough for a couple of pints, as it maintained a hotel license. Marlborough House is a Category C Listed Building on the British Listed Buildings website.

James and Annie moved north to live and work in Aberdeen. Daughter Anne Paterson Clark was born on 7 August 1927 at 70 Forest Avenue, St Machar, Aberdeen, to father James Paterson Clark, a commercial traveller, and mother Annie Black Cameron. James Paterson Clark, 68, died in 1965 in Aberdeen Southern district.

Neale's paternal great-grandparents – George Cooper and Emma Crory Black

Neale's other paternal great-grandfather George Cooper was born around 1863 in Old Machar, Aberdeen, Aberdeenshire, to father John Cooper, a cabinet maker, and mother Isabella Watt. In 1871, George, 8, a scholar, resided at Nellfield Place, Old Machar, Aberdeen, with father John Cooper, 38, a cabinet maker, mother Isabella, 32, (b. ~1839, Aberdeen), his siblings John, 5, a scholar, Nelly, 3, Rachel, 2, and a lodger Robert Gordon, 27, another cabinet maker. His paternal great-grandmother Emma Crory Black was born on 17 February 1871 in Dromore, Banbridge, County Down, Ireland to father William Black, a public house proprietor, and mother Jane Tait (or Tate). George Cooper, a furniture upholstery journeyman, married Emma Crory Black on 6 July 1893 in Belfast, County Antrim, Ireland in the 4th Quarter 1893 (Belfast Registration District Volume 1).

George and Emma lived and worked in Belfast until around 1897, when they moved to Aberdeen. They had 6 known children, although one died in infancy; in Belfast, Isabella (b. ~1895), in Aberdeen, William John (b. 10 March 1897), Emma J (b. ~1900), George (b. ~1901) and James B (b. ~1908). Their son William John Cooper was born on 10 March 1897 at 60 Broomhill Road, Old Machar, Aberdeen. In 1911, George Cooper, 48, an upholsterer, resided at 250 Union Grove, Holburn, Aberdeen, with his wife Emma, 40, children Isabella, 16, a grocery clerkess, William J, 14, Emma J, 11, George, 10, and James B, 3. George Cooper, 57, an upholsterer journeyman, died in 1920 at St Machar, Aberdeen. By 1935, George's widow Emma was proprietor of two properties at 74 & 76-Mile End Avenue, Aberdeen. As WWII came to an end, Emma Crory Cooper nee Black, 74, of 76 Mile End Avenue, Aberdeen died on 27 February 1945 at 5 Albyn Place, Aberdeen of complete procidentia uteri, for 20 years, complicated by an operation and coronary thrombosis as certified by Dr C S Davidson FRCS.

The death was registered by her married daughter Isabella Gordon, of 76 Mile End Avenue, Aberdeen, on 1 March 1945 at the Aberdeen Registry Office.

Neale's paternal great-grandparents – John Quin and Emmeline Holland

Neale's other paternal great-grandfather John Quin and his great-grandmother Emmeline Holland were probably born around 1872. Daughter Emmeline Frances Quin was born in 1899 in Penicuik, Midlothian to father John Quin, a commercial traveller, and mother Emmeline Holland. Emmeline Quin nee Holland, 70, died in 1942, during WWII, in Penicuik, Midlothian. John Quin, 82, died in 1955 in Haymarket, Edinburgh.

Neale's maternal great-grandparents – Adam Clark and Agnes Paterson

Neale's maternal great-grandfather Adam Clark was born around 1861 and great-grandmother Agnes Paterson was born around 1865, both in Glasgow's east end. Adam Clark, a patternmaker, married wife Agnes Paterson on 20 February 1891 in Camlachie, Glasgow. They had four known children in Glasgow; Isabella Paterson (b. ~1893), Adam (b. ~1894), James Paterson (b. 10

December 1896) and John A (b. ~1899). Their son James Paterson Clark was born on 10 December 1896 at 330 Saracen Street, Possilpark, Glasgow. In 1911, Adam Clark, 49, an instrument maker's patternmaker, resided at 215 Saracen Street, Possilpark, Glasgow, with wife Agnes, 46, children Isabella P, 18, a typist for an insurance firm, Adam, 17, a general clerk for a tobacco manufacturer, James P, 14, an office boy in a ship's brokerage, and John A, 12, at school. Adam Clark, 79, died in 1940, during WWII, in Cathcart, Glasgow. Agnes Clark nee Paterson, 84, died in 1949 in Cathcart.

Neale's other maternal great-grandparents – William Cameron and Susan Black

Neale's maternal great-grandfather William Cameron was born around 1843 in Kilmallie, Inverness-shire and his great-grandmother Susan Black was born around 1857 in Greenock, Renfrewshire. It should be noted that Neale Cooper has two separate and unrelated Black lineages in his ancestry. Around 1877, Susan Black married a first husband surnamed Lindsay and she had a daughter Susan Lindsay (b. ~1879, Kinning Park). However, by 1885, Susan was widowed.

William Cameron, a schoolmaster, married wife Susan Black in 1885 in Paisley, Renfrewshire, and they had 6 known children in Glasgow, all baptized in St

Enoch's Free Church, Waterloo Street; Elizabeth (b. 14 December 1885), William Kennedy (b. 27 March 1887), Sarah McGregor (b. 2 September 1888), twins Flora and Helen Graham (b. 2 November 1890) and Annie Black (b. 13 September 1894). In 1891, William Cameron, 48, a teacher in a public school, resided at 5 Inverarity Garden Terrace, Partick, Glasgow, with wife Susan, 34, a teacher's wife, step-daughter Susan Lindsay, 12, a scholar, children Elizabeth, 5, William, 4, Sarah, 2, and twins Flora and Helen, 6 months old. Also living at William's home was Catherine Smith, 20, a general domestic servant. William spoke Gaelic and English.

Daughter Annie Black Cameron was born on 13 September 1894 in Glasgow to father William Cameron, a schoolmaster, and mother Susan Black. She was baptized in St Enoch's Free Church of Scotland. William's wife Susan, 37, died shortly after childbirth in 1894 in Partick, Glasgow. In the 1905–06 Post Office Directory for Glasgow, William Cameron, residing at 33 Partickhill Road, Partick, a substantial blond sandstone terrace apartment, was a schoolmaster at Dowanhill Public School, Partick. The Dowanhill Public School is a fine Victorian red sandstone Grade C Listed Building erected around 1894–96. William Cameron, a retired schoolmaster, residing at 76 Mossgiel Road, Newlands, Glasgow, was still alive in 1924. Mossgiel Road is a smart row of Edwardian pink sandstone terraced homes and Newlands was distinctly upmarket during William Cameron's era. William Cameron, 82, died the following year in 1925 in Cathcart, Glasgow.

Neale's paternal great-great-grandparents – John Cooper and Isabella Watt

Neale's paternal great-great-grandfather John Cooper was born around 1833 in Kincardine O'Neil in Aberdeenshire and great-great-grandmother Isabella Watt was born around 1839 in Aberdeen, Aberdeenshire. In 1861, John Cooper, 28, a cabinet maker, resided at Hardgate, Old Machar, with his mother Hellen, 59, his step-brother Alexander Coutts, 35, a shop porter, and his niece Ann Coutts, 6, a scholar.

John Cooper, a cabinet maker, married his wife Isabella Watt on 1 August 1862 in Old Machar, Aberdeen. John and Isabella had 4 known children in Aberdeen; George (b. ~1863), John (b. ~1866), Helen aka Nelly (b. ~1868) and Rachel (b. ~1869). In 1871, John Cooper, 38, a cabinet maker, resided at Nellfield Place, Old Machar, Aberdeen, with his wife Isabella, 32, children George, 8, a scholar, John, 5, a scholar, Nelly, 3, Rachel, 2, and a lodger Robert Gordon, 27, another cabinet maker. John Cooper was dead by 1907 and his wife Isabella Cooper nee Watt, 71, died in St Machar, Aberdeen in 1909.

Neale's paternal great-great-grandparents – William Black and Jane Tate

Neale's other paternal great-great-grandfather William Black was born around 1838 in Anahilt, County Down, Ireland. His great-great-grandmother Jane Tate (or Tait) was born around 1840 in County Down. William Black married Jane Tate and they had a known daughter Emma. Daughter Emma Crory Black was born on 17 February 1871 in Dromore, Banbridge, County Down to father William Black, a public house proprietor, and mother Jane Tait. In an article entitled *'A Short History of Public Houses in Dromore'* by Will Patterson published in the Dromore Historical Journal, William Black is listed as a spirit dealer in Market Square, Dromore, but he is not listed as a publican in Dromore in Bassett's County Down Directory in 1886. William Black, a public house proprietor, and his wife Jane were dead by 1945.

Chapter 5:

Alex McLeish (Centre half)
Honours as an Aberdeen player:
1 European Cup Winners Cup
1 European Super Cup
3 Scottish League titles
5 Scottish Cups
2 Scottish League Cups

The young Alex McLeish

Alexander McLeish aka Alex was born on 21 January 1959 in Duke Street Hospital, Dennistoun, Glasgow to father Alexander Nimmo McLeish, a Clyde shipyard worker, and mother Jean McDonald Wylie. At that time the McLeish family lived at 118 Bernard Street, Bridgeton, Glasgow. As a boy, McLeish supported Glasgow Rangers, a team he would later successfully manage. McLeish is a Scottish professional football manager and former player. He played in the central defensive area for Aberdeen during their 1980s glory years, making nearly 500 league appearances for the club.

PRIDE OF THE DONS

After living in the Parkhead and Kinning Park districts of Glasgow, the family moved to Barrhead, Renfrewshire soon after McLeish reached school age. He attended Springhill Primary, then Barrhead High School – where he was one year below future Aberdeen and Scotland teammate Peter Weir – and finally John Neilson High School in Paisley. As a juvenile he played for Barrhead Youth Club, alongside Weir, and Glasgow United. He also trained for a short period with Hamilton Academicals. After a local cup final with Glasgow United in 1976 watched by an Aberdeen delegation, including then manager Ally MacLeod, McLeish signed for the Pittodrie club the following day.

McLeish spent the majority of his first two seasons at Aberdeen in the reserves and also had a loan spell at local junior team Lewis United. He made his competitive debut for manager Billy McNeill in a New Year fixture against Dundee United on 2 January 1978. His first major final appearance was under manager Alex Ferguson as a substitute in a 2–1 loss to Rangers in the 1978–79 League Cup. Most of his appearances during the late 1970s were as a midfielder, with Willie Garner and Doug Rougvie preferred in the defence. However, McLeish eventually made the centre-half position his own, and over the next seven seasons he enjoyed significant success, winning eight domestic and two European trophies. Highlights included scoring in a 4–1 victory over Rangers in the 1982 Scottish Cup Final on his 200th Dons appearance. He also scored a vital goal against Bayern Munich during the campaign leading to the

European Cup Winners' Cup win over Real Madrid in 1983. During this period, McLeish formed a formidable defensive triumvirate with Willie Miller and Jim Leighton for both club and country. He also won 77 caps for Scotland. Even after he had won his first Scotland cap, McLeish's father asked Aberdeen boss Ferguson to persuade him to continue with accountancy training. When Ferguson left in 1986 to go to Manchester United, he tried to sign McLeish, but the deal fell through. He won Scottish player of the year in 1990, after a season when Aberdeen won both domestic cups. He became captain of Aberdeen after Willie Miller retired. His 692 competitive appearances for the Dons rank second-highest in its history, behind his old compatriot Miller.

Alex's parents – Alexander Nimmo McLeish and Jean McDonald Wylie

As the dark storm clouds of war gathered across Europe, Alex's father Alexander Nimmo McLeish aka Alex was born on 19 June 1938 at 246 Dunn Street, Bridgeton, Glasgow to a father also named Alexander Nimmo McLeish, a carpenter's labourer, and mother Mary Lamont. The birth was registered by his father Alex McLeish on 1 July 1938 at the Glasgow Registry Office. On the day Alex's mother Jean was born, the Armistice of 22 June 1940, during WWII, was signed at Compiègne, France, by officials of Nazi Germany and the Third French Republic. On Adolf Hitler's orders this took place at the same location and in the same railway carriage that the Germans surrendered on 11 November 1918. Jane McDonald Wylie aka Jean was born on 22 June 1940 at 24 Martin Street, Bridgeton, Glasgow to father Thomas Wylie, an iron dresser, and mother Jessie Johnstone McDonald. The birth was registered by Jean's father Thomas Wylie on 1 July 1940 at the Glasgow Registry Office.

Alexander Nimmo McLeish, 20, a ship plater, of 59 Leithland Road, Pollok, Glasgow, married wife Jane McDonald Wylie, 18, a book binder, of 299 Househillwood Road, Pollok, Glasgow, on 11 July 1958 at St James Pollok Church according to the Church of Scotland. The wedding was conducted by Rev James Currie, minister of St James Pollok; the best man was James Mallon and the bridesmaid was Margaret Quinn.

Reverend James Currie was a larger-than-life character, well known for his uplifting preaching, intelligence, and sense of humour. Currie appeared on many religious TV programmes such as *The Epilogue* and *Late Call*. The author, who was raised in Pollok in the 1970s, remembers Jimmy Currie well. He was at his cousin Robert McNeill's wedding to Catherine Curran at St James, where the Reverend Currie officiated.

Alex and Jean's son Alexander McLeish was born on 21 January 1959 in the Duke Street Hospital, Dennistoun, Glasgow to his father Alexander Nimmo

McLeish, a shipyard worker, and to his mother Jean McDonald Wylie. At that time Alex and Jean lived at 118 Bernard Street, Bridgeton, Glasgow. They were listed in the 1959 Electoral Register for the Burgh of Glasgow, Bridgeton district, 3rd Municipal Ward as follows: -

656: 118 Bernard Street: Alexander McLeish

657: 118 Bernard Street: Jean McLeish

Alex and Jean were still living there in 1961, but most of Bernard Street was condemned in 1962. The family moved to Kinning Park on Glasgow's south side, followed by a move to Barrhead, Renfrewshire a few years later.

Alex's paternal grandparents – Alexander Nimmo McLeish and Mary Lamont

Alex's paternal grandfather Alexander Nimmo McLeish aka Alex was born on 1 August 1905 at No.19 Nuneaton Street, Bridgeton, Glasgow to his father John McLeish, a weaving factory twister, and mother Isabella Anderson. The birth was registered by mother Isabella McLeish on 23 August 1905 at Glasgow Registry Office.

In 1911, Alexander, 5, at school, resided at No.3 Delburn Street, Camlachie, Glasgow, with his father John McLeish, 36, a yarn winder in a weaving factory, his mother Isabella, 37, and his other siblings. In 1924, Alexander Nimmo McLeish, 19, enlisted in the Royal Air Force, as recorded in catalogue AIR 79 at National Archives, Kew, London.

Alex's paternal grandmother Mary Lamont was born about 1912, possibly in Glasgow, to father George Lamont, a general labourer, and mother Jean Smith. Alexander Nimmo McLeish, 26, a general labourer, of 20 Delburn Street, Parkhead, Glasgow, married Mary Lamont, 20, a cotton weaver, of 36 Dunn Street, Bridgeton, Glasgow, on 30 September 1932 in St Francis in the East Church according to Church of Scotland. The wedding was conducted by Rev H R Warnes, minister of St Francis in the East; the best man was Andrew McLeish, Alex's brother, and the bridesmaid was Mary McLeish, Alex's sister.

Son Alexander Nimmo McLeish aka Alex was born on 19 June 1938 at 246 Dunn Street, Bridgeton, Glasgow to father Alexander Nimmo McLeish, a carpenter's labourer, and mother Mary Lamont. The birth was registered by his father Alex McLeish on 1 July 1938 at the Glasgow Registry Office. Alexander Nimmo McLeish, 64, a commission agent's clerk, died in 1969 in Glasgow. His wife Mary McLeish nee Lamont, 86, died in 1999 in Glasgow.

Alex's maternal grandparents – Thomas Wylie and Jessie Johnstone McDonald

Alex's maternal grandfather Thomas Wylie was born on 30 December 1911 at 30 Martin Street, Bridgeton, Glasgow to father James Wylie, a foundry labourer, and mother Margaret Jane Devlin. The birth was registered by Thomas's father James Wylie on 5 January 1912 at the Glasgow Registry Office. Alex's maternal grandmother Jessie Johnstone McDonald was born around 1915 in Bridgeton, Glasgow to his father Malcolm McDonald, a riveter's holder-on, and mother Margaret White.

Thomas Wylie, 21, an iron dresser, of 24 Martin Street, Bridgeton, Glasgow, married Jessie Johnstone McDonald, 18, a chemical worker, of 44 Norman Street, Bridgeton, Glasgow, on 16 June 1933 at the Sacred Heart Church, Bridgeton according to the Roman Catholic Church. The wedding was conducted by Fr Anthony Mullins, priest at the Sacred Heart Church; the best man was Neil Steen and the bridesmaid was Mary Donohue.

As an aside, Fr Anthony Mullins also married Robert Murdoch and Barbara MacDonald on 31 December 1943, as detailed in the author's book *Pride of the Lions*. Their son Bobby Murdoch became one of the famous Lisbon Lions who lifted the European Cup in 1967. Fr Anthony Mullins officiated at two weddings, whose unions led to the creation of two giants of Scottish and European football.

PRIDE OF THE DONS

Daughter Jane McDonald Wylie aka Jean was born on 22 June 1940 at 24 Martin Street, Bridgeton, Glasgow to father Thomas Wylie, an iron dresser, and mother Jessie Johnstone McDonald. The birth was registered by Jean's father Thomas Wylie on 1 July 1940 at the Glasgow Registry Office. Thomas Wylie, 62, died in 1974 in Glasgow. His wife Jessie Johnstone Wylie nee McDonald, 78, died in 1993 in Barrhead, Renfrewshire.

Alex's paternal great-grandparents – John McLeish and Isabella Anderson

Alex's paternal great-grandfather John McLeish was born around 1875, probably in Glasgow, to father John McLeish, a cotton weaver, and mother Elizabeth Malcolm. His great-grandmother Isabella Anderson was born around 1874, probably in Glasgow, to father David Anderson, a blacksmith, and his mother Annie Barrie. John McLeish, 18, a weaving factory twister, of 432 London Road, Bridgeton, Glasgow, married Isabella Anderson, 19, a cotton weaver, of 357 Lord Darnley Street, Strathbungo, Glasgow, on 28 April 1893 at the Anderson family home according to the Church of Scotland. The wedding was conducted by Rev George Allan, minister of Newlands Parish Church; the best man was James Hamilton and the bridesmaid was Mary McGuire.

John and Isabella had 9 known children in Glasgow, one having died in infancy; John (b. ~1894), Charles (b. ~1896), James (b. ~1899), Thomas (b. ~1901), Robert (b. ~1904), Alexander (b. 1 August 1905), William (b. ~1909) and Annie (b. ~1911). Their son Alexander Nimmo McLeish aka Alex was born on 1 August 1905 at 19 Nuneaton Street, Bridgeton, Glasgow to his father John McLeish, a weaving factory twister, and mother Isabella Anderson. The birth was registered by mother Isabella McLeish on 23 August 1905 at Glasgow Registry Office.

In 1911, John McLeish, 36, a yarn winder in a weaving factory, resided at 3 Delburn Street, Camlachie, Glasgow, with wife Isabella, 37, children John, 17 a yarn in-giver, Charles, 15, a yarn in-giver, James, 12, Thomas, 10, Robert, 7, Alexander, 5, all at school, William, 2, and Annie, 4 months old. John McLeish, a yarn twister, and wife Isabella were still alive in 1932 at 20 Delburn Street, Camlachie, Glasgow. John McLeish, 63, died in 1938 and his wife Isabella McLeish nee Anderson, 67, died in 1941, during WWII, both in Shettleston, Glasgow.

Alex's paternal great-grandparents – George Lamont and Jean Smith

Alex's other paternal great-grandfather George Lamont and his great grandmother Jean Smith were born around 1875, possibly in Glasgow. George Lamont, a general labourer, married Jean Smith and they had a daughter Mary Lamont born about 1912, also probably in Glasgow. George Lamont, a general labourer, was dead by 1932, however, his wife Jean was still alive.

Alex's maternal great-grandparents – James Wylie and Margaret Jane Devlin

Alex's maternal great-grandfather James Wylie was born around 1876 in Belfast, Co. Antrim, Ireland to father Alexander Wylie, a carter, and his mother Ann McKillen. His great-grandmother Margaret Jane Devlin (or Devline) was born around 1879 in Glasgow to father Hugh Devlin, a chemical work labourer, and mother Sarah McMurray. James Wylie, 20, an iron foundry labourer, of 3 Broomhill Street, Blythswood, Glasgow, married Margaret Devlin, 17, an earthenware transferrer, of 9 Broomhill Street, Blythswood, Glasgow, on 17 July 1896 at St Aloysius Chapel, Garnethill, Glasgow, according to the RC Church. The wedding was conducted by Fr William Lawson; the best man was Henry Devlin, Margaret's brother, and the bridesmaid was Mary Walls.

James and Margaret had 3 known sons in Glasgow; Alexander aka Alex (b. ~1899), Hugh (b. ~1901) and Thomas (b. 30 December 1911). In 1901, James Wylie, 24, an iron foundry labourer, resided at 9 Broomhill

Street, St Rollox, Barony, Glasgow, with wife Margaret, 22, and sons, Alex, 2, Hugh, 4 months old. His in-laws Hugh and Sarah also lived up the same close at that time. Son Thomas Wylie was born on 30 December 1911 at 30 Martin Street, Bridgeton, Glasgow to his father James Wylie, a foundry labourer, and his mother Margaret Jane Devlin. The birth was registered by Thomas's father James Wylie on 5 January 1912 at the Glasgow Registry Office. James Wylie, an iron foundry labourer, and wife Margaret were still alive in 1933 in Bridgeton, Glasgow. James Wylie, 80, a retired foundry labourer, married to Margaret Jane Devlin, died on 7 September 1956, at 24 Martin Street, Bridgeton, Glasgow, of cerebral thrombosis and hypostatic pneumonia as certified by Dr Arthur Jamieson MB ChB. The death was registered by son Alex Wylie, of 44 Dunragit Street, Dennistoun, Glasgow, on 8 September 1956 at Glasgow Registry Office. Margaret Jane Wylie nee Devlin, 87, died in 1965 in Glasgow.

Alex's other maternal great-grandparents – Malcolm McDonald and Margaret White

Alex's maternal great-grandfather Malcolm McDonald and his great-grandmother Margaret White were born around 1880, possibly in Glasgow. Malcolm McDonald, a riveter's holder-on in the Clyde shipbuilding industry, married Margaret White.

Malcolm and Margaret had a daughter Jessie Johnstone McDonald born around 1915 in Bridgeton, Glasgow. Malcolm McDonald, a riveter's holder-on, and wife Margaret were still alive in 1933 in Bridgeton, Glasgow.

Alex's paternal great-great-grandparents – John McLeish and Elizabeth Malcolm

Alex's paternal great-great-grandfather John McLeish and his great-great-grandmother Elizabeth Malcolm were born around 1845, probably in Glasgow. John McLeish, a cotton weaver, married wife Elizabeth Malcolm and they had a son John (b. ~1875), probably in Glasgow. Elizabeth McLeish nee Malcolm, 45, died in 1892 in Blackfriars, Glasgow. John McLeish, a cotton weaver, was still alive in 1893.

Alex's other paternal great-great-grandparents – David Anderson and Annie Barrie

Alex's other paternal great-great-grandfather David Anderson and great-great-grandmother Annie Barrie were born around 1850, probably in Glasgow. David Anderson, a blacksmith, married Annie Barrie and they had a daughter Isabella (b. ~1874), probably in Glasgow. David Anderson, a blacksmith, and wife Annie were still alive in 1893 in Strathbungo, Glasgow.

Alex's maternal great-great-grandparents – Alexander Wylie and Ann McKillen

Alex's maternal great-great-grandfather were Alexander Wylie and great-great-grandmother Ann McKillen (or McKellen) both born around 1850, in County Antrim, Ireland. Alexander Wylie, a carter, married Ann McKillen and they had 4 known children in Belfast; Margaret Ellen (b. 25 November 1874), James (b. ~1876), Mary (b. 5 March 1879) and Ann (b. 28 July 1880). Daughter Mary Wylie was baptized on 11 March 1879 in St Patrick's Roman Catholic Church, Birch Street, Belfast. Alexander Wylie, a carter, and wife Ann were still alive in 1896.

Alex's maternal great-great-grandparents – Hugh Devlin and Sarah McMurray

Alex's other maternal great-great-grandfather Hugh Devlin (or Devline), son of Hugh Devlin, was born around 1836 and great-great-grandmother Sarah McMurray (or McMurry), daughter of John McMurray, was born around 1844, both in County Londonderry,

Ireland. Hugh and Sarah both lived through the devastating Irish Potato Famine (1846-52). Hugh Devlin married Sarah McMurray on 21 November 1864 in Magherafelt, County Londonderry. Hugh and Sarah had 7 known children; James (b. 9 October 1865, Coagh, Tyrone); in Glasgow, Mary Ann (b. 25 March 1867), Elizabeth (b. 31 March 1868), Henry (b. 26 June 1869), Catherine (b. 30 March 1872), then Margaret Jane (b. ~1879) and Sarah (b. ~1881).

Hugh Devlin, a chemical work labourer, wife Sarah and son James had emigrated to Glasgow around 1866. In 1901, Hugh Devlin, 65, a chemical labourer, resided at 9 Broomhill Street, St Rollox, Barony, Glasgow, with wife Sarah, 57, son James, 35, a chemical labourer, and daughter Sarah, 20, a book-folder. Also living up the same close was son-in-law James Wylie, 24, an iron foundry labourer, their daughter Margaret, 22, and his grandsons, Alex, 2, Hugh, 4 months old. Sarah Devlin nee McMurray, 72, died in 1916 in Bridgeton, Glasgow.

Alex's maternal great-great-great-grandfathers – Hugh Devlin and John McMurray

Alex's maternal great-great-great-grandfathers Hugh Devlin (or Devline) and John McMurray (or McMurry) were born around 1810, probably in County Londonderry, Ireland.

DEREK NIVEN

Hugh Devlin had a son Hugh (b. ~1840) and John McMurray had a daughter Sarah (b. ~1840), both in County Londonderry. Both Hugh Devlin and John McMurray were still alive in 1864 in County Londonderry, Ireland.

Chapter 6:

Willie Miller MBE (left half)
Honours as an Aberdeen player:
1 European Cup Winners Cup
1 European Super Cup
3 Scottish League titles
4 Scottish Cups
3 Scottish League Cups

The young Willie Miller

Sir Alex Ferguson once described Willie Miller as "the best penalty box defender in the world". William Ferguson Miller was born on 2 May 1955 at 253 Leslie Street, Pollokshields, Glasgow to his father William Andrews Miller, an engineer's toolmaker, and mother Jean McLaren Milne. The birth was registered by father William Miller on 21 May 1955 at the Glasgow Registry Office. At that time the Miller family resided at No.156 Marquis Street, Bridgeton, Glasgow.

Miller was raised in Bridgeton in Glasgow's east end. He is a Scottish professional football player and manager, who registered a club record of 560 league appearances for Aberdeen. Miller had no interest in football as a young child, and when he did become drawn to the game he initially played as a goalkeeper. He was scouted by several professional clubs while playing at forward with Glasgow Schools and Eastercraigs Boys Club. Having been on unofficial schoolboy terms in 1969, Miller, 16, signed full-time for Aberdeen in 1971 and spent a season on loan with Peterhead in the Highland League, scoring 24 goals. Upon Miller's return to Pittodrie he was converted to a central defender / sweeper in the reserves on Teddy Scott's advice. Miller soon established himself in that position in the first team replacing Henning Boel. By 1975 he had been made team captain by manager Ally MacLeod.

Miller's central defensive partnership with Alex McLeish was integral to Aberdeen's success in the 1980s. He won all the major domestic trophies and the European Cup Winners' Cup and Super Cup in 1983. He made a record 560 league appearances for Aberdeen in 14 consecutive seasons. He amassed a total of 12 trophies, as well as appearing in several other finals. His total of 797 competitive appearances for the club is comfortably (by more than 100 matches) the all-time record. Miller won 65 international caps for Scotland between 1975 and 1989, scoring one goal. His 50th cap came against West Germany during the 1986 FIFA World Cup. He retired from playing in 1990 due to an injury picked up whilst playing for Scotland in the last qualifying game for the 1990 FIFA World Cup. A farewell testimonial match in his honour took place in December 1990 with Aberdeen facing a 'World Cup XI' (featuring amongst other players Kenny Dalglish, David O'Leary, Mark Hughes and Danny McGrain) at Pittodrie Stadium. Miller had also previously received another testimonial in 1981 against Tottenham Hotspur. In 2003, Willie Miller was voted the greatest Aberdeen player of all time in a poll to mark the club's centenary. In 2015, it was no surprise when he was named in Aberdeen's 'greatest ever team' by the supporters' club.

Willie's parents – William Andrews Miller and Jean McLaren Milne

Willie's father William Andrews Miller was born on 1 October 1929 at 13 Marquis Street, Bridgeton, Glasgow to father Hugh Miller, a foundry labourer, and mother Agnes Walker Ferguson. The birth was registered by his father Hugh Miller on 18 October 1929 at the Glasgow Registry Office. Six days later in New York, the Wall Street Crash on 24 October 1929 heralded the start of the 10 year worldwide economic downturn known as the Great Depression. The Great Depression and postwar Germany's economic and political crises also saw Nazi Führer Adolf Hitler's rise to power in 1933. That same year, Willie's mother Jean McLaren Milne was born on 20 September 1933 at 21 Dale Street, Bridgeton, Glasgow to father Andrew Ross Milne, a meat market labourer, and mother Jeanie McLaren. The birth was registered by her father A R Milne on 9 October 1933 at the Glasgow Registry Office.

William Andrews Miller, 24, an engine fitter journeyman, of 13 Marquis Street, Bridgeton, Glasgow, married Jean McLaren Milne, 20, of 119 Bernard Street, Bridgeton, Glasgow, on 22 January 1954 at St Francis in the East Church according to the Church of Scotland. The wedding was conducted by Rev John C Sim, minister of St Francis in the East; the witnesses were A Milne, Jean's brother, and T MacKenzie. William and Jean had 4 known children in Bridgeton, Glasgow. Son William Ferguson Miller was born on 2 May 1955 at 253 Leslie Street, Pollokshields in Glasgow to his father William Andrews Miller, an engineer's toolmaker, and mother Jean McLaren Milne. Son Graham McLaren Miller was born on 13 November 1956 at 76 Bernard Street, Bridgeton, Glasgow. Son Brian Whitelaw Miller was born on 5 September 1959 at 76 Bernard Street, Bridgeton, Glasgow. Daughter Jean Hyslop Miller was born on 20 September 1963 at 43 Marquis Street, Bridgeton, Glasgow. During the late 1960s, William and Jean's marriage broke down and in 1971 Jean filed for a divorce. In a Register of Corrected Entries for the district of Bridgeton (RCE 1079/1971/GLW) dated 18 August 1971 in Edinburgh, Jean Milne or Miller was granted a divorce against William Andrews Miller on 11 June 1971.

Willie's paternal grandparents – Hugh Miller and Agnes Walker Ferguson

Willie's paternal grandfather Hugh Miller (or Millar) was born on 7 December 1906 at High Craigends, Kilsyth, Stirlingshire, to father William Miller, a coal miner, and mother Christina Andrews. Hugh was registered as Hugh Millar by his father who signed as *William Millar* on 17 December 1906 at Kilsyth Registry Office. Willie's paternal grandmother Agnes Walker Ferguson was born in 1908 in Camlachie, Glasgow to father Fergus Ferguson, a carter, and mother Martha Walker. In 1911, Hugh, 4, resided at 45 High Craigends, Kilsyth, with his father William Millar, 45, an ironstone miner hewer, mother Christina, 45, a tailoress, and his other siblings.

Hugh, who signed as *Hugh Miller*, 21, a general labourer, married Agnes Ferguson, 21, a shirt machinist, both of 31 Soho Street, Camlachie, Glasgow, on 30 May 1929 at 44 Overtoun Drive, Rutherglen according to the Church of Scotland. The wedding was conducted by Rev Robert Jack, minister of Chalmers Parish Church, Glasgow; the best man was Donald Pearson and the bridesmaid was Elizabeth Ferguson, Agnes' sister. Son William Andrews Miller was born on 1 October 1929 at 13 Marquis Street, Bridgeton, Glasgow to father Hugh Miller, a foundry labourer, and mother Agnes Ferguson.

The birth was registered by his father Hugh Miller on 18 October 1929 at Glasgow Registry Office. Hugh Miller, a builder's labourer, and his wife Agnes were both alive in Bridgeton, Glasgow in 1954.

Willie's maternal grandparents – Andrew Ross Milne and Jeanie McLaren

On 28 June 1914, anarchist Bosnian-Serb student Gavrilo Princip assassinated Austrian Archduke Franz Ferdinand in Sarajevo, sparking the outbreak of the Great War. Two days later, Willie's maternal grandfather Andrew Ross Milne was born on 30 June 1914 at 105 Cumberland Street, Calton, Glasgow, to his father William Bain Milne, a confectionery packer, and mother Annie Knowles Ross. The birth was registered by father W B Milne on 15 July 1914 at Glasgow Registry Office. Willie's maternal grandmother Jeanie McLaren was born around 1913 in Glasgow to father John McLaren, a bricklayer, and mother Jeanie McKellar.

After leaving school Andrew got a job at the huge Glasgow Meat Market in the Bellgrove district of Glasgow. Andrew Ross Milne, 18, a meat market labourer, of 94 Arcadia Street, Calton, Glasgow, married wife Jeanie McLaren, 19, a hosiery factory worker, of 10 Savoy Street, Bridgeton, Glasgow, on 18 April 1933 at 320 London Road, Calton, Glasgow, by warrant of the

Sheriff Substitute of Lanarkshire in a civil ceremony. The best man was Archibald Mitchell and the bridesmaid was Jeanie Paterson Brogan or Mitchell, both of No.17 Little Dovehill, Calton, Glasgow. Daughter Jean McLaren Milne was born on 20 September 1933 at 21 Dale Street, Bridgeton, Glasgow to father Andrew Ross Milne, a meat market labourer, and his mother Jeanie McLaren. The birth was registered by her father A R Milne on 9 October 1933 at the Glasgow Registry Office. Andrew Ross Milne, 55, a retired clerk, died in 1970 in Glasgow. His wife Jeanie Milne nee McLaren, 70, died in 1984 also in Glasgow.

Willie's paternal great-grandparents – William Miller and Christina Andrews

Willie's paternal great-grandfather William Miller (or Millar) was born illegitimately on April Fools' Day, 1 April 1866 at Backbrae, Kilsyth to mother Barbara Black Miller, a cotton weaver. The birth was registered by his mother Barbara Miller, who signed with her 'x' mark, on 16 April 1866 at the Kilsyth Registry Office. Willie's great-grandmother Christina Andrews was born around 1865, in Dullatur, near Cumbernauld in Lanarkshire, to father Henry Andrews, an ironstone miner, and mother Christina Donaldson.

William Miller, 24, a coal miner, who signed as *William Millar*, of 64 Main Street, Kilsyth, married wife Christina Andrews, 25, a cotton weaver, of High Craigends, Kilsyth, on 4 April 1890 according to the Kilsyth Congregational Church. The wedding was conducted by Rev J C Hodge; the best man was Hugh McWhinney and the bridesmaid was Jessie Harper Hamilton. William and Christina had 8 known children in Kilsyth; Christina (b. ~1891), Andrew (b. ~1893), John (b. ~1895), Henry (b. ~1897), Mary (b. ~1899), William (b. ~1902), James (b. ~1905) and Hugh (b. 7 December 1906).

Son Hugh Miller (or Millar) was born on 7 December 1906 at High Craigends, Kilsyth, Stirlingshire, to father William Miller, a coal miner, and his mother Christina Andrews. Hugh was registered as Hugh Millar by his father and William again signed as *William Millar* on 17 December 1906 at the Kilsyth Registry Office. In 1911, again signed as William Millar, 45, an ironstone miner hewer, resided at 45 High Craigends, Kilsyth, with wife Christina, 45, a tailoress, children Christina, 20, a tailoress, Andrew, 18, John, 16, both ironstone miners, Henry, 14, a horse keeper below ground, Mary, 12, William, 9, James, 6, all at school, and Hugh, 4. William Miller, a coal miner, and wife Christina were both alive in 1929. Christina Miller nee Andrews, 75, died in 1940, during WWII, in Camlachie, Glasgow.

Willie's other paternal great-grandparents – Fergus Ferguson and Martha Walker

Willie's other paternal great-grandfather Fergus Ferguson and his great-grandmother Martha Walker were born around 1865, possibly in Glasgow. Fergus Ferguson, a carter, married Martha Walker in 1892 in Dennistoun, Glasgow. Their daughter Agnes Walker Ferguson was born in 1908 in Camlachie, Glasgow to father Fergus Ferguson, a carter, and mother Martha Walker. Fergus Ferguson, a carter, and wife Martha were both dead by 1929.

Willie's maternal great-grandparents – William Bain Milne and Annie Knowles Ross

Willie's maternal great-grandfather William Bain Milne was born in 1869 in St Andrew parish, Dundee to father James Milne, a mill overseer, and mother Agnes Bain. His great-grandmother Annie Knowles Ross was born around 1874 probably in Dundee to father James Ross, a lorryman, and mother Margery aka Marjory Knowles. William Bain Milne, 24, a van man, married Annie Knowles Ross, 19, a powerloom weaver, both of 77 Centre Street, Tradeston, Glasgow, on 2 November 1894 at No.10 Guildry Court, Glasgow according to the Free Church of Scotland. The wedding was conducted by Rev James Duff McCulloch; the best man was Alexander Ross, Annie's brother, and the bridesmaid was

Annie McDonald. James Duff McCulloch was born in 1836 in Logie Easter, Ross and Cromarty. He studied divinity at New College, Edinburgh and was licensed as a Free Church minister in 1867. In 1889 he was minister at Hope Street Free Gaelic Church in Glasgow and became the second Moderator of the General Assembly in 1901/02.

Son Andrew Ross Milne was born on 30 June 1914 at 105 Cumberland Street, Calton, Glasgow, to his father William Bain Milne, a confectionery packer, and mother Annie Knowles Ross. The birth was registered by his father W B Milne on 15 July 1914 at the Glasgow Registry Office. William Bain Milne, 66, a confectionery packer, died in 1937 in Camlachie, Glasgow. His wife Annie Knowles Milne nee Ross, 69, died in 1945 in Bridgeton, Glasgow.

Willie's maternal great-grandparents – John McLaren and Jeanie McKellar

Willie's other maternal great-grandfather John McLaren and great-grandmother Jeanie McKellar were born around 1880 possibly in Glasgow. John McLaren, a bricklayer, married Jeanie McKellar in 1911 in St Rollox, Glasgow. Daughter Jeanie McLaren was born around 1913 in Glasgow to father John McLaren, a bricklayer, and mother Jeanie McKellar.

John McLaren, a bricklayer, and wife Jeanie were both still alive in Glasgow in 1933.

Willie's paternal great-great-grandmother – Barbara Black Miller

Willie's paternal great-great-grandmother was Barbara Black Miller born on Christmas Day, 25 December 1836 in Kilsyth, Stirlingshire to her father James Miller, a weaver, and mother Janet Miller. Her father James died between 1837 and 1841. In 1841, Barbara, 6, lived in Backbrae, Kilsyth with her widowed mother Janet Miller, 41, a hand-loom weaver, and her siblings. In 1851, Barbara, 13, a scholar, was still living at Backbrae, Kilsyth, with her widowed mother Janet Miller, 50, a weaver, and her siblings, all working as weavers. After leaving school, Barbara also became a cotton weaver.

In 1861, Barbara, 21, a cotton weaver, still resided at Backbrae, Kilsyth, with her mother Janet, 64, a tambourer, and her sister Margaret, 24, a cotton weaver. Barbara Miller, a cotton weaver, gave birth to her son William Miller, who was born illegitimately on April Fools' Day, 1 April 1866 at Backbrae, Kilsyth. The birth was registered by his mother Barbara Miller, who signed with her 'x' mark, on 16 April 1866 at Kilsyth Registry Office. Given that Barbara did not use her father's name for her only son, it is possible the errant father was named William, as women commonly used this ploy to shame them. Barbara Miller or Millar, stated as 60, although closer to 67, never married, died in 1903 in Kilsyth, where she had lived all her life.

Willie's paternal great-great-grandparents – Henry Andrews and Christina Donaldson

Willie's other paternal great-great-grandparents Henry Andrews and Christina Donaldson were born around 1825, possibly in Kilsyth, Stirlingshire. Henry Andrews, an ironstone miner, married Christina Donaldson on 17 May 1851 in Kilsyth and they had a daughter Christina born around 1865 in Dullatur, near Cumbernauld, Lanarkshire. Henry Andrews, 55, an ironstone miner, died in 1890 in Kilsyth. Henry's wife Christina Andrews nee Donaldson, 72, died in 1907 also in Kilsyth.

Willie's maternal great-great-grandparents – James Milne and Agnes Bain

Willie's maternal great-great-grandparents James Milne and Agnes Bain were born around 1840, possibly in Dundee, Forfarshire. James Milne, a mill overseer, married Agnes Bain in 1868 in St Peter parish,

Dundee and son William Bain Milne was born in 1869 in St Andrew parish, Dundee. James Milne, a mill overseer, and wife Agnes were still alive in 1894 in Dundee.

Willie's maternal great-great-grandparents – James Ross and Margery Knowles

Willie's other maternal great-great-grandparents James Ross and Margery aka Marjory Knowles were born around 1850, possibly in Dundee. James Ross, a lorryman, married Marjory Knowles in 1874 in Lochee, Dundee and daughter Annie Knowles Ross was born around 1874 in Dundee. James Ross, a lorryman, and wife Margery were still alive in Dundee in 1894.

Willie's paternal great-great-great-grandparents – James Miller and Janet Miller

Willie's paternal great-great-great-grandfather James Miller and great-great-great-grandmother Janet Miller were born around 1797 in Kilsyth, Stirlingshire. It is likely that Janet had an illegitimate son James Rennie around 1821 in Kilsyth. James Miller, a weaver, married Janet Miller on 15 September 1828 in Kilsyth. They had 4 known children in Kilsyth; Jean (b. ~1829), John (b. ~1832), Margaret (b. ~1834) and Barbara Black (b. 25 December 1836). It is likely that James Miller died between 1837 and 1841. In 1841, Janet Miller, 41, a widowed hand loom weaver, resided in Backbrae, Kilsyth with her five children James Rennie, 20, Jean Miller, 12, John, 9, Margaret, 7, and Barbara, 6, along with six Irish labourers as boarders to supplement Janet's meagre income. In 1851, Janet Miller, 50, a widowed weaver, still resided at Backbrae, Kilsyth, with children James Rennie, 30, a weaver, Jean Miller, 21, a weaver, John, 18, a weaver, Margaret, 15, a weaver, and Barbara, 13, a scholar. Janet became a skilled tambourer, a type of embroiderer who stretched cotton over a tambour. In 1861, Janet Miller, 64, a tambourer, still resided at Backbrae, Kilsyth, with daughters Margaret, 24, a cotton weaver, Barbara, 21, a cotton weaver, and boarder Henry Brichen, 13, a cotton weaver. Janet Miller, 75, died in 1872 in Kilsyth.

Chapter 7:

Gordon Strachan OBE (Outside Right)
(This chapter is also published in Pride of the Jocks by Derek Niven)
Honours as an Aberdeen player:
1 European Cup Winners Cup
1 European Super Cup
2 Scottish League titles
3 Scottish Cups

The young Gordon Strachan

Gordon David Strachan was born on 9 February 1957 in the Eastern General Hospital, Leith to his father James Gordon Strachan and mother Catherine Livingstone Carse. Gordon was raised in a suburban housing scheme at 24 West Pilton Circus, Muirhouse, Edinburgh. Father Jim worked as a tubular scaffolder and mother Catherine worked in a whisky distillery. As a young boy, Strachan supported Hibernian.

DEREK NIVEN

At age 15, he damaged his vision playing football on the school playground when a pen became lodged in his right eye, almost costing him his sight. Strachan was initially offered a contract by Hibernian manager Eddie Turnbull, but his father Jim refused it. Strachan played for Dundee, Aberdeen, Manchester United, Leeds United, Coventry City and Scotland. In international football he earned 50 caps, appearing in two World Cup finals; Spain 1982 and Mexico 1986. Aged 40, Strachan retired from playing in 1997, setting a Premier League record for an outfield player.

Strachan's managerial career started in 1996 with Coventry City and Southampton. After resigning in February 2004, he took a 16-month hiatus. Strachan returned to management on 1 June 2005, replacing Irishman Martin O'Neill as Celtic manager. After a less than impressive start at Parkhead, Strachan coached Celtic to victory in the League Cup. In April 2006 Celtic won the Scottish Premier League title. Two consecutive league titles followed in 2006-07 and 2007-08. Under Strachan, Celtic also won the Scottish League Cup twice in 2006 and 2009 and the Scottish Cup in 2007. Strachan signed for Middlesbrough on 26 October 2009, but after poor results, he left on 18 October 2010. He was appointed Scotland national team manager on 15 January 2013, succeeding Craig Levein. However, the national side's qualification for a major tournament since Craig Brown took Scotland to the 1998 World Cup eluded Strachan.

PRIDE OF THE DONS

He narrowly missed taking the Scots to the 2014 World Cup and Euro 2016. After failing to qualify for the 2018 World Cup, Strachan resigned on 12 October 2017.

Gordon's parents – James Gordon Strachan and Catherine Livingstone Carse

Gordon's father James Gordon Strachan was born around 1936 in Canongate, Edinburgh, to father Alexander Strachan, a postman, and mother Bridget Rafferty. Gordon's mother Catherine Livingstone Carse was also born around 1936 in Edinburgh to father David Wright Carse, a railway capstanman, and mother Jane Duncan. James Gordon Strachan, 19, a sawmill labourer, of 50 Granton Crescent, Edinburgh, married Catherine Livingstone Carse, 20, of No.24 West Pilton Circus, Muirhouse, Edinburgh on 10 March 1956 at Granton Congregational Church, Boswall Parkway, Edinburgh. The wedding was conducted by Rev B A Cox; the best man was J S Nichol and the bridesmaid was Isobel Carse, Catherine's sister. Jim and Catherine moved to 24 West Pilton Circus, Muirhouse, Edinburgh and Jim worked as a tubular scaffolder. Their son Gordon David Strachan was born on 9 February 1957 in the Eastern General Hospital, Leith.

Gordon's paternal grandparents – Alexander Strachan and Bridget Rafferty

Gordon's paternal grandfather Alexander Strachan was actually born Alexander Lundie Lamb on 5 September 1902 at the Royal Maternity Hospital, Edinburgh to father George Lamb, a coal salesman, and mother Agnes Slimman. The birth was registered by mother Agnes Lamb, of 50 Bristo Street, Edinburgh. Alexander never knew his father George as he died on 9 April 1902. Gordon's grandmother, Bridget Rafferty, was born around 1905, probably in Edinburgh, to father Michael Rafferty, a general labourer, and mother Mary Ann Lavin. By the time Alexander got married to Bridget in 1929, he was working as a postman for the General Post Office, and he was then called Alexander Strachan. Alexander Strachan, 26, a postman, of 3 St John's Hill, Edinburgh, married Bridget Lafferty, 24, a laundress, of 80 Canongate, Edinburgh, on 10 May 1929 at 11 Royal Terrace, Edinburgh. The wedding was conducted by Rev Archibald Morrison, minister of Abbey Parish Church; the witnesses were Joseph and Catherine Donoghue. Son James Gordon Strachan was born in 1936 in Canongate, Edinburgh, to his father Alexander Strachan, a postman, and his mother Bridget Rafferty. Alexander Strachan, a postman, was dead by 1956, however, his wife Bridget Strachan nee Rafferty was still alive by then.

Gordon's maternal grandparents – David Wright Carse and Jane Duncan

Gordon's maternal grandfather David Wright Carse and his grandmother Jane Duncan were born around 1910 probably in Edinburgh. David and Jane had two known daughters in Edinburgh; Catherine Livingstone (b. ~1936) and Isobel. David Wright Carse worked as a railway capstanman, with the London & North Eastern Railway Company. David Carse was responsible for shunting wagons around the LNER goods depot. In 1947, he was transferred to British Railways under the post-war Labour government's nationalisation scheme. David Wright Carse, a railway capstanman, and his wife Jane Carse nee Duncan were both still alive in Muirhouse, Edinburgh in 1956.

Gordon's paternal great-grandparents – George Lamb and Agnes Slimman

Gordon's paternal great-grandfather George Lamb was born around 1879 in Edinburgh, to father Charles James Lamb, a coal carter, and his mother Elizabeth Kerr. George became a brewer's cellarman before becoming a coal carter like his father. Gordon's great-grandmother Agnes Slimman was born around 1882 in Edinburgh to her father Charles Slimman, a grocer, and her mother Agnes Lundie.

On 21 July 1896 George Lamb, only 17, had registered the death of his father Charles from heart disease at Edinburgh Registry Office. George Lamb, 22, a brewer's cellarman, of 105 Dundee Street, Edinburgh, married Agnes Slimman, 19, of 91 Dundee Street, Edinburgh, on 17 May 1901 at All Saints Church, Brougham Street, Edinburgh. The wedding was conducted by Fr Alex D Murdoch, Episcopal priest; the witnesses were J S Nichol, Colin Campbell and Mary Slimman, Agnes's sister. In early 1902, Agnes fell pregnant but just weeks later tragedy struck, when her husband George had a massive heart attack. This was possibly genetically inherited from his father Charles, who also died young of heart disease. George Lamb, only 23, a coal carter, of No.59 Lauriston Street, Edinburgh, died on 9 April 1902 at Edinburgh Royal Infirmary of cardiac asystole, aortic stenosis and incompetence for three months as certified by Dr Ian S Stewart MB. The death was registered by June Tripp, George's aunt, of 16 Eglinton Street. Five months after his father's death, Alexander Lundie Lamb was born on 5 September 1902 at the Royal Maternity Hospital, Edinburgh, as registered by George's widow Agnes Lamb, of 50 Bristo Street, Edinburgh. Agnes, who remarried, later changed her son's name to Alexander Strachan. Agnes Lamb nee Slimman was still alive in 1929.

Gordon's other paternal great-grandparents – Michael Rafferty and Mary Ann Lavin

Gordon's paternal great-grandfather Michael Rafferty and his great-grandmother Mary Ann Lavin were born around 1875 probably in Edinburgh, although, almost certainly of Irish descent. Michael and Mary Ann had a known daughter Bridget (b. ~1905) probably in Edinburgh. Michael Rafferty, a general labourer, and his wife Mary Ann Rafferty nee Lavin were still alive in 1929.

Gordon's paternal great-great-grandparents – Charles James Lamb and Elizabeth Kerr

Gordon's paternal great-great-grandfather Charles James Lamb was born on 1 July 1856 in Edinburgh, to father Thomas Lamb, aka George, a stone quarryman, and mother Margaret Brown. His great-grandmother Elizabeth Kerr was born around 1856, probably in Edinburgh. Charles and Elizabeth had three known children in St George's, Edinburgh; George (b. ~1879), Mary Ann Bellinger (b. 18 May 1881) and Benjamin Bellinger McPherson (b. 17 July 1891). Charles Lamb, a coal carter, died at West Port, Edinburgh on 21 July 1896 of mitral heart disease, for two years, and pneumonia, for seven days, as certified by Dr Robert A Fleming MD. Elizabeth Lamb nee Kerr, 66, died in Edinburgh in 1920.

Gordon's paternal great-great-grandparents – Charles Slimman and Agnes Lundie

Gordon's other paternal great-great-grandfather Charles Slimman and his great-great-grandmother Agnes Lundie were born around 1855. Charles and wife Agnes had two known daughters in Edinburgh; Agnes (b. ~1882) and Mary. Charles Slimman, a grocer, and his mother Agnes Slimman nee Lundie were both alive in Edinburgh in 1901.

Gordon's paternal great-great-great-grandparents – Thomas Lamb and Margaret Brown

Gordon's paternal great-great-great-grandfather Thomas Lamb, also known as George, and his great-great-great-grandmother Margaret Brown were born around 1820 probably in Edinburgh. Thomas and Margaret had four known children in Edinburgh; Charles (b. 1 July 1856), George Fotheringham (b. 23 April 1858), Thomas Henry (b. 14 May 1860) and Margaret Isabella (b. 23 April 1862). Thomas recorded as George Lamb, a stone quarryman, and his mother Margaret Lamb nee Brown were dead by 1896.

Chapter 8:

Neil Simpson (inside right)
Honours as an Aberdeen player:
1 European Cup Winners Cup
1 European Super Cup
2 Scottish League titles
3 Scottish Cups
1 Scottish League Cup

The young Neil Simpson

Neil Alexander Simpson was born on 15 November 1961 in Hackney, London, England to mother Sheila Margaret Simpson, working as a nursing sister, who had moved down from Aberdeenshire to work in London. Neil's birth was registered in November 1961 (Hackney 5C/751). He is a Scottish former footballer, who played for Aberdeen, Newcastle United, Motherwell and Scotland. Simpson, nicknamed "Simmie", was born in London to his Scottish mother and they soon moved back to New Machar in their native Aberdeenshire, where he was raised at 14 Summer Brae.

DEREK NIVEN

Joining his boyhood club Aberdeen in 1980 from local junior side Middlefield Wasps, he made 310 appearances in all competitions including 27 as a substitute and he scored 31 goals. Between 1982 and 1986, Simpson's Pittodrie career earned him domestic winner's medals including two Scottish League championships, three Scottish Cups and a Scottish League Cup. Simpson played in the 1981–82 UEFA Cup campaign. This saw the Dons make their first-ever run of success in Europe by progressing to the third round at the expense of Bobby Robson's Ipswich Town and FC Argeş Piteşti of Romania.

In 1982–83, he played in every match of the Dons' 1983 European Cup Winners Cup campaign. He scored a goal in the 3–2 victory over Bayern Munich in the second leg of the quarter-finals. Simpson became one of the "Gothenburg Greats" who lifted the trophy after beating Real Madrid 2–1 in the 1983 Final. Just a few weeks later after his momentous victory, Neil, still living at 14 Summer Brae, New Machar, married his wife Elaine on 11 June 1983 at Dyce Parish Church according to the Church of Scotland. The wedding was conducted by Rev James P Scott, minister of Dyce Parish Church.

The following season, Simpson was in the team that reached the semi-finals of the 1984 European Cup Winners Cup. He also scored when Aberdeen won the 1983 UEFA Super Cup. In 1985–86, he helped the team to the quarter-finals of the 1986 European Champions Cup.

PRIDE OF THE DONS

In October 1988, Simpson made a dreadful tackle that injured Ian Durrant leaving the Rangers player out of action for two and a half years. This increased the hostility between both clubs' supporters, which still exists over 30 years later. In 1993, Simpson and Durrant settled out of court for an undisclosed sum after Durrant sued for damages. Simpson's injury problems continued, restricting him to nine league appearances in 1989–90 and a move to Newcastle United saw him play only four games. He transferred to Motherwell in 1991–92 where he spent two seasons before leaving for Highland Football League side Cove Rangers. He ended his playing career in October 1993. Simpson was awarded a testimonial match by Aberdeen, played against an Alex Ferguson Manchester United XI on 14 August 2012.

Neil's mother – Sheila Margaret Simpson

Neil's mother Sheila Margaret Simpson was born on 27 August 1936 in Cloves, Alves, Morayshire, to father Frederick George Simpson, a farm servant, and mother Joan Thomson. The birth was registered by her father Frederick G Simpson on 15 September 1936 at Alves Registry Office. After schooling, Sheila enrolled in nursing and by 1960 she was a nursing sister living and working in Hackney, London. In the spring of 1961 Sheila fell pregnant and gave birth to her son Neil Alexander Simpson, who was born on 15 November 1961 in Hackney, London. Neil's father is unknown and due to the circumstances, Sheila returned with her baby son Neil to New Machar, Aberdeenshire, where she raised him. When Neil was 14, Sheila met Edward Milne, a bus driver, and they married in 1975. Sheila Margaret Simpson, 38, a nursing sister, of 14 Summer Brae, New Machar, married Edward James Sinclair Milne, 30, an omnibus driver, of 53 King Street, Peterhead on 22 February 1975 at New Machar Parish Church. Sheila and husband Edward had a son Ewan, Neil's stepbrother. Sheila Margaret Milne nee Simpson, 83, died in 2020 in Peterhead registered by her son Ewan Milne.

Neil's maternal grandparents – Frederick George Simpson and Joan Thomson

Neil's paternal grandfather Frederick George Simpson was born on Christmas Eve, 24 December 1906 at West Balthangie Farm, Monquhitter, Aberdeenshire to father Frederick Simpson, a farm servant, and mother Lizzie Calder. The birth was registered by his father Frederick Simpson on Boxing Day 26 December 1906 at the Monquhitter Registry Office. Neil's paternal grandmother Joan Thomson was born on 25 June 1906 at Russell's Buildings, Rothney, Aberdeenshire to father John Thomson, a farm servant, and mother Elizabeth Riddell. The birth was registered by her father John Thomson on 7 July 1906 at the Premnay Registry Office.

Frederick George Simpson, 22, a farm servant, of Newcraig, Udny, married Joan Thomson, 22, a domestic servant, of Upper Brackla, Premnay, on 1 February 1929 at Randwick, Rothney, Premnay according to the Church of Scotland. The wedding was conducted by Rev Andrew Burt BD, minister of Insch; the best man was Keith Paterson and the bridesmaid was Jeannie Ann Walker. By 1934, Frederick and Joan lived in Miltonhill, Alves, Morayshire. Daughter Sheila Margaret Simpson was born on 27 August 1936 in Cloves, Alves, Morayshire, to father Frederick George Simpson, a farm servant, and mother Joan Thomson. The birth was registered by her father Frederick G Simpson on 15 September 1936 at the Alves Registry Office. Joan Simpson nee Thomson, 90, died in 1996 in Bucksburn, Aberdeenshire.

Neil's maternal great-grandparents – Frederick Simpson and Eliza Paterson McKay Calder

Neil's maternal great-grandfather Frederick Simpson was born on 28 March 1878 at Cairnbanno, New Deer, Aberdeenshire to father Alexander Simpson, a farmer, and mother Isabella Robb. The birth was registered by his father Alexander Simpson on 17 March 1878 at the New Deer Registry Office. Neil's great-grandmother Eliza Paterson McKay Calder, aka Lizzie, was born illegitimately on 9 September 1886 in the Maud Poorhouse, New Deer to mother Mary Calder, a domestic servant. The birth was registered by her mother Mary Calder on 29 September 1886 at the New Deer Registry Office. Mary, who was then in the Old Deer Poorhouse, raised an action for a paternity suit against the father of repute David McKay with the Sheriff Substitute of Aberdeenshire and Banff and it was recorded in a Register of Corrected Entries, as follows: -

RCE 225/1/120 - insert the name David McKay on the authority of a certificate in an action of paternity of a female child born at Maud Poorhouse at the instance of Poor Mary Calder inmate of the Combination Poorhouse Old Deer against David McKay Mains of Coldwells on the 1st day of December 1886.

Frederick Simpson, 25, a ploughman, of Grassiehill, New Deer, married Lizzie Calder, 18, a domestic servant, of Bank Village, Maud, on 9 December 1904 at Smart's Hall, New Deer according to the Church of Scotland. The wedding was conducted by the Rev William Adams, minister of New Deer; the best man was Edward Simpson, Frederick's brother, and the bridesmaid was Mary Fraser. Son Frederick George Simpson was born on Christmas Eve 24 December 1906 at West Balthangie Farm, Monquhitter, Aberdeenshire to father Frederick Simpson, a farm servant, and mother Lizzie Calder. The birth was registered by father Frederick Simpson on Boxing Day 26 December 1906 at Monquhitter Registry Office.

Between 1915 and 1920, Frederick Simpson was a tenant at the Mains Estate of Asleid, Monquhitter. Frederick Simpson, a farm servant, and his wife Lizzie were both still alive in 1929.

Neil's maternal great-grandparents – John Thomson and Elizabeth Riddell

Neil's other maternal great-grandfather John Thomson was born illegitimately around 1878 in the county of Aberdeenshire to father John Thomson, a blacksmith, and mother Maggie Bremner. Neil's great-grandmother Elizabeth Riddell (or Riddel or Riddle) was born around 1874 in Aberdeenshire. John Thomson, 28, a farm servant, of Oakhill, Old Meldrum, married Elizabeth Riddell, 32, a domestic servant, of Kennethmont, on 2 June 1906 at Victoria Cottage, Rothney according to the Church of Scotland. Daughter Joan Thomson was born on 25 June 1906 at Russell's Buildings, Rothney, Aberdeenshire to father John Thomson, a farm servant, and mother Elizabeth Riddell. The birth was registered by her father John Thomson on 7 July 1906 at the Premnay Registry Office. John Thomson, a farm servant, was dead by 1929, although wife Elizabeth was still alive then.

Neil's maternal great-great-grandparents – Alexander Simpson and Isabella Robb

Neil's maternal great-great-grandfather Alexander Simpson was born around 1821 in New Deer, Aberdeenshire to his father Alexander Simpson, a farmer, and mother Christian Milne. Neil's great-great-grandmother Isabella Robb was born around 1834 in Aberdeenshire to father James Robb, an agricultural labourer, and her mother Christian Scott. In 1861, Alexander Simpson, 40, a farmer of 24 acres, resided at the croft house of Burnthill, Cairnbanno, New Deer, with widowed mother Christian, 66, nieces Mary Davidson, 10, a scholar, Christian Johnstone, 1, and George Robertson, 14, a farm servant. Alexander Simpson, stated as 39, a farmer, of Cairnbanno, New Deer, married Isabella Robb, 27, a domestic servant, also of Cairnbanno, on 17 November 1863 at Cairnbanno Farm according to the Church of Scotland. The wedding was conducted by Rev John Stevenson, minister of Millbrex; the witnesses were James Robb and John Johnston.

Alexander and Isabella had 2 known sons at Cairnbanno; Edward and Frederick (b. 28 March 1878). Son Frederick Simpson was born on 28 March 1878 at Cairnbanno, New Deer to father Alexander Simpson, a farmer, and mother Isabella Robb. The birth was registered by father Alexander Simpson on 17 March 1878 at the New Deer Registry Office. In 1885, farmer Alexander Simpson was a tenant in Burnthill croft house, Cairnbanno Estate.

Alexander Simpson, a farmer, died in 1896 in New Deer, although his wife Isabella was still alive in 1904.

Neil's maternal great-great-grandparents – David McKay and Mary Calder

Neil's maternal great-great-grandfather of repute David McKay and great-great-grandmother Mary Calder were born around 1860 in Aberdeenshire. Their illegitimate daughter Eliza Paterson McKay Calder, aka Lizzie, was born on 9 September 1886 in the Maud Poorhouse, New Deer to her mother Mary Calder, a domestic servant. The birth was registered by her mother Mary Calder on 29 September 1886 at the New Deer Registry Office. David McKay was named in a paternity suit raised by Mary Calder, residing in the Old Deer Poorhouse, in Aberdeen Sheriff Court on 1 December 1886. Mary Calder, a domestic servant, who never married, was still alive in 1904.

Neil's maternal great-great-grandparents – John Thomson and Maggie Bremner

Neil's other maternal great-great-grandfather John Thomson and his great-great-grandmother Maggie Bremner were born around 1850 in Aberdeenshire.

Their illegitimate son John Thomson was born around 1878 in Aberdeenshire to father John Thomson, a blacksmith, and mother Maggie Bremner. John and Maggie never married, however, Maggie later married George Ross, a farmer. John Thomson, a blacksmith, and wife Maggie Ross nee Bremner were both alive in 1906.

Neil's maternal great-great-great-grandparents – Alexander Simpson and Christian Milne

Neil's maternal great-great-great-grandfather Alexander Simpson was born around 1783 and great-great-great-grandmother Christian Milne was born around 1789 in Monquhitter, Aberdeenshire. Alexander Simpson, an agricultural labourer, married Christian Milne around 1820 and they had four known children; Alexander (b. ~1824), Christian (b. ~1830), Ann (b. ~1832) and Helen (b. ~1835). In 1841, Alexander Simpson, 59, an agricultural labourer, resided at Cairnbanno, New Deer, with wife Christian, 50, daughters Christian, 11, Ann, 9, and Helen, 6. In 1855, farmer Alexander Simpson was a tenant in Burnthill croft house, Auchmunziel, Cairnbanno. Alexander Simpson, 77, a farmer, died in 1859 in New Deer. In 1861, Christian, 66, a widow, resided at Cairnbanno, New Deer, with son Alexander Simpson, 40, a farmer of 24 acres, and her granddaughters Mary Davidson, 10, a scholar, and Christian Johnstone, 1. Christian Simpson nee Milne, 77, died in 1877 in New Deer.

Neil's maternal great-great-great-grandparents – James Robb and Christian Scott

Neil's other maternal great-great-great-grandfather James Robb and great-great-great-grandmother Christian Scott were born around 1800 in Aberdeenshire. James Robb, an agricultural labourer, married Christian Scott and had a daughter Isabella (b. ~1834). James Robb, an agricultural labourer, and his wife Christian were still alive in 1863. Christian Robb nee Scott, 84, died in 1885 in Old Deer.

Chapter 9:

Mark McGhee (centre forward)
Honours as an Aberdeen player:
1 European Cup Winners Cup
1 European Super Cup
2 Scottish League titles
3 Scottish Cups

The young Mark McGhee

Mark Edward McGhee was born on 25 May 1957 in Rottenrow Maternity Hospital, Townhead, Glasgow, to father Edward McGhee, a television engineer, and mother Mary Jordan Farrel. The birth was registered by his father Edward McGhee on 29 May 1957 at the Glasgow Registry Office. At the time the family lived at 85 Springfield Road, Parkhead, Glasgow, in the shadow of Celtic Park. The family were big Celtic fans. McGhee is a Scottish professional football player, coach and manager.

PRIDE OF THE DONS

McGhee started his career at Greenock Morton in 1975 and had spells at clubs including Newcastle United, Aberdeen, Hamburger SV, Glasgow Celtic, IK Brage and Reading. McGhee was part of the Aberdeen side that won the 1983 European Cup Winners' Cup and 1983 UEFA Super Cup. After retiring from playing, he managed several clubs in England and Scotland, including Reading, Millwall, Aberdeen and Brighton & Hove Albion. McGhee began his professional career in 1975 at Morton, where he became a promising centre-forward. In December 1977 he moved to England, signing for Newcastle United. Despite an encouraging start at St James' Park, managerial changes saw McGhee fall out of favour. McGhee returned north in March 1979 as Alex Ferguson's first major signing for Aberdeen.

He debuted for the Dons on 1 April 1979 against former club Morton. He won his first major honour the following season when Aberdeen won the Scottish Premier Division. This was the first time in 15 years that a club outside the Old Firm had finished Scottish Champions. At Pittodrie, McGhee won a further league title in 1984 as well as a hat-trick of successive Scottish Cup wins from 1982 to 1984. He was an integral part of the 1983 Aberdeen side that defeated Real Madrid 2–1 in the European Cup Winners' Cup final. His extra-time cross from the left set up John Hewitt to score the winning goal. McGhee also won the European Super Cup the following season, scoring against Hamburg SV in the second leg at Pittodrie. During his Aberdeen career, he also won Scottish PFA Players' Player of the Year in 1982.

Mark's parents – Edward McGhee and Mary Jordan Farrel

Mark's father Edward McGhee was born on 1 February 1930 at 5 Braidfauld Street, Shettleston, Glasgow, to father James McGhee, a coal miner, and mother Annie McConville. The birth was registered by his father James McGhee on 3 February 1930 at the Glasgow Registry Office. After leaving school, Edward joined the rail industry prior to nationalisation in 1947 and was a locomotive brakesman for the London and North Eastern Railway Company. Mark's mother Mary Jordan Farrel was born on 27 June 1934 at 22 Battleburn Street, Shettleston, Glasgow, to father Charles Farrel, a tube worker, and mother Elizabeth Wilson Corrie. The birth was registered by her father Charles Farrel on 5 July at the Glasgow Registry Office. After leaving school, Mary got a job as a carpet finisher.

Edward McGhee, 22, a locomotive brakesman, of 15 Easterhill Place, Tollcross, Glasgow, married Mary Jordan Farrel, 18, a carpet finisher, of 45 Potter Street, Tollcross, Glasgow, on 28 June 1952 at the Good Shepherd Church, Shettleston, Glasgow, according to the RC Church. The wedding was conducted by Rev Father Vincent O'Sullivan, Catholic clergyman; the best man was Edward's brother John McGhee, of 15 Easterhill Place, Glasgow, and the bridesmaid was Mary's sister Jenny Farrel, of 45 Potter Street, Glasgow. Their son Mark Edward McGhee was born on 25 May 1957 in Rottenrow Maternity Hospital, Townhead, Glasgow, to his father Edward McGhee, a television engineer, and mother Mary Jordan Farrel. The birth was registered by his father Edward McGhee on 29 May 1957 at the Glasgow Registry Office. At the time the family lived at 85 Springfield Road, Parkhead, Glasgow.

Mark's paternal grandparents – James McGhee and Annie McConville

Mark's paternal grandfather James McGhee was born on 11 February 1890 at 65 Main Street, Tollcross, Lanarkshire to father John McGhee, a steel worker, and mother Rose Ann Gunn. The birth was registered by his father John McGhee on 17 February 1890 at Shettleston Registry Office. In 1891, James, 14 months old, resided at 65 Main Street, Tollcross, with father John McGhee, 31, a fireclay miner, and mother Rose Ann, 27. Mark's paternal grandmother Annie McConville was born around 1891 in Old Monkland, Lanarkshire to father John McConville, a coal miner, and mother Rose Ann Smith. James McGhee, 33, a coal miner, of 91 Causewayside, Tollcross, Glasgow, married Annie McConville, 32, of 5 Braidfauld Street, Glasgow, on 14 July 1923 at St Joseph's RC Church, Tollcross according to the Roman Catholic Church.

The wedding was conducted by Fr Matthew Quillinan, RC clergyman; the best man was James McConville, Annie's brother, and the bridesmaid was June McGhee, James's sister. James and Annie had 2 known sons in Tollcross; John and Edward (b. 1 February 1930). Son Edward McGhee was born on 1 February 1930 at 5 Braidfauld Street, Glasgow, to father James McGhee, a coal miner, and mother Annie McConville. The birth was registered by his father James McGhee on 3 February 1930 at the Glasgow Registry Office. James McGhee, a coal miner, and his wife Annie were still alive in 1952.

Mark's maternal grandparents – Charles Farrel and Elizabeth Wilson Corrie

Mark's maternal grandfather Charles Farrel was born around 1900 in Tollcross, Glasgow to father James Farrel, a tube worker, and mother Mary Jordan. After leaving school, Charles, like his father James, worked as a tube worker at the huge Stewarts & Lloyds Tube Works. The company was founded in 1903 by the amalgamation of two of Britain's largest iron and steel manufacturers. In 1921, Charles, 20, a draw benchman at Stewarts & Lloyds, resided at 10 Lloyd's Avenue, Tollcross, with his father James Farrel, 49, a tube furnaceman at Stewarts & Lloyds Tube Works, mother Mary, 45, a house domestic, and his other siblings.

PRIDE OF THE DONS

His grandmother Elizabeth Wilson Corrie was born around 1904 in Tollcross, Glasgow to father John Corrie, a tube worker, and mother Elizabeth Tennant. In 1921, Elizabeth, 17, a cloth finisher at James Park's Bleachworks in Carmyle, resided at 7 Lloyd's Avenue, Tollcross, with her father John Corrie, 36, a steel tube worker at Stuart & Lloyd's Tube Works, her mother Elizabeth, 36, a house domestic, and her other siblings.

Charles Farrel, 24, a tube worker, of 10 Lloyds Avenue, Tollcross, married Elizabeth Wilson Corrie, 20, of 7 Lloyds Avenue, Tollcross, on 28 January 1924 at St Joseph's RC Church according to the RC Church. The wedding was conducted by Fr Peter Fitzpatrick, RC clergyman; the best man was James Farrel, Charles's brother, and the bridesmaid was Margaret Mary Smith.

Charles and Elizabeth had 2 known daughters in Tollcross; Mary Jordan (b. ~1934) and Jenny. Their daughter Mary Jordan Farrel was born on 27 June 1934 at 22 Battleburn Street, Shettleston, Glasgow, to father Charles Farrel, a tube worker, and mother Elizabeth Wilson Corrie. The birth was registered by her father Charles Farrel on 5 July at the Glasgow Registry Office. Charles Farrel, a locomotive brakesman, and his wife Elizabeth were still alive in 1952.

Mark's paternal great-grandparents – John McGhee and Rose Ann Gunn

Mark's paternal great-grandfather John McGhee (or McGee) was born on 9 December 1859 in Tollcross, Lanarkshire to father James McGhee, a mason's labourer, and mother Jane Lafferty. The birth was registered by his father James McGhee, who signed with his 'x' mark, on 11 December 1859 at the Shettleston Registry Office. In 1861, John, 1, resided at Peter Love's Land, Shettleston, with his father James McGhee, 30, a labourer, mother Jane, 23, a housekeeper, and his brother James, 2 months old. In 1881, John, 20, a coal miner, resided at New Signs, Causewayside Street, Tollcross, with his father James McGhee, 53, a coal mine labourer, his mother Jane, 44, and his other siblings. Mark's great-grandmother Rose Ann Gunn was born around 1864 in Shotts, Lanarkshire to father Felix Gunn, a furnaceman, and mother Mary McCabe. When Rose Ann left school, she became a power loom weaver.

John McGhee, 28, a coal miner, of 141 Main Street, Tollcross, married Rose Ann Gunn, 24, a power loom weaver, of Easterhill Street, Tollcross, on 8 November 1888 at St Paul's RC Church according to the Roman Catholic Church. The wedding was conducted by Fr Joseph van Hecke; the best man was Edward McGhee, John's brother, and the bridesmaid was Mary McGuire. Just a few months earlier, newly-founded Glasgow Celtic played its first match on 8 May 1888, a friendly against Rangers, winning 5-2.

John and Rose had 2 known children; James (b. 11 February 1890) and June. Son James McGhee was born on 11 February 1890 at 65 Main Street, Tollcross, Lanarkshire to father John McGhee, a steel worker, and mother Rose Ann Gunn. The birth was registered by his father John McGhee on 17 February 1890 at Shettleston Registry Office.

In 1891, John McGhee, 31, a fireclay miner, resided at 65 Main Street, Tollcross, with wife Rose Ann, 27, son James, 14 months old, and a lodger Bernard McNish, 22, a boilermaker. John McGhee, a coal miner, was dead by 1923, however, his wife Rose Ann was still alive by then.

Mark's paternal great-grandparents – John McConville and Rose Ann Smith

Mark's other paternal great-grandfather John McConville and his great-grandmother Rose Ann Smith were born around 1865 in Lanarkshire. John McConville, a coal miner, married Rose Ann Smith and they had 2 known children; James and Annie (b. ~1891). John McConville, a coal miner, was dead by 1923, however, his wife Rose Ann was still alive by then.

Mark's maternal great-grandparents – James Farrel and Mary Jordan

Mark's maternal great-grandfather James Farrel was born around 1872 and his great-grandmother Mary Jordan was born around 1876, both in Bothwell, Lanarkshire. James Farrel, a tube worker, married Mary Jordan around 1898 and they had 9 known children; in Bothwell, James (b. ~1898), Charles (b. ~1900); in Tollcross, Glasgow, Daniel (b. ~1903), Arthur (b. ~1904), Edward (b. ~1906), Cornelius (b. ~1908), Laurence (b. ~1910), Mary (b. ~1913) and Elizabeth (b. ~1915). In 1921, James Farrel, 49, a tube furnaceman at Stewarts & Lloyds Tube Works, resided at 10 Lloyd's Avenue, Tollcross, with wife Mary, 45, a house domestic, children James, 22, Charles, 20, both draw benchmen at Stewarts & Lloyds, Daniel, 18, a checker for the North British Railway Company, Arthur, 17, Edward, 15, both message boys for Tollcross Cooperative Society, Cornelius, 13, Laurence, 11, Mary, 8, and Elizabeth, 6, all at school. James Farrel, a tube worker, and wife Mary were still alive in 1924.

Mark's maternal great-grandparents – John Corrie and Elizabeth Tennant

Mark's other maternal great-grandfather John Corrie and his great-grandmother Elizabeth Tennant were born around 1885 in Old Monkland, Lanarkshire.

John Corrie, a tube worker, married Elizabeth Tennant around 1904 and they had nine known children; in Tollcross, Elizabeth Wilson (b. ~1904); in Old Monkland, James (b. ~1908); in Tollcross, Janet (b. ~1909), Walter (b. ~1912), John (b. ~1914); back in Old Monkland, Sybell (b. ~1916), Thomas (b. ~1919), Robert (b. ~1920) and Grace (b. ~1921). In 1921, John Corrie, 36, a steel tube worker at Stewarts & Lloyds Tube Works, resided at 7 Lloyd's Avenue, Tollcross, with wife Elizabeth, 36, a house domestic, children Elizabeth, 17, a cloth finisher at James Park's Bleachworks in Carmyle, James, 13, Janet, 12, Walter, 9, John, 7, Sybell, 5, all at school, Thomas, 2, Robert, 1, and Grace, 3 months old. John Corrie, a tube worker, and wife Elizabeth were still alive in 1924.

Mark's paternal great-great-grandparents – James McGhee and Jane Lafferty

Mark's paternal great-great-grandfather James McGhee (or McGee) was born around 1830 and his great-great-grandmother Jane Lafferty was born around 1837, both in Ireland. James and Jane married on 1 February 1859 in Shettleston and they had eleven known children in Tollcross; John (b. 9 December 1859), James (b. 28 January 1861), Edward (b. ~1863), Mary (b. ~1864), Bridget (b. ~1867), Thomas (b. ~1868), Margaret (b. ~1869), Catherine (b. ~1872), Jane (b. ~1874), Francis (b. ~1876) and Patrick (b. ~1879).

DEREK NIVEN

Son John McGhee (or McGee) was born on 9 December 1859 in Tollcross, Lanarkshire to father James McGhee, a mason's labourer, and mother Jane Lafferty. The birth was registered by his father James McGhee, who signed with his 'x' mark, on 11 December 1859 at the Shettleston Registry Office. Son James McGhee (or McGee) was born on 28 January 1861 in Tollcross, Lanarkshire to father James McGhee, a coal labourer, and mother Jane Lafferty. The birth was registered by father James McGhee, who signed with his 'x' mark, on 31 January 1861 at the Shettleston Registry Office.

In 1861, James McGhee, 30, a labourer, resided at Peter Love's Land, Shettleston, with wife Jane, 23, a housekeeper, sons John, 1, and James, 2 months old. His next-door neighbour was his Irish-born brother John McGhee, 27, an agricultural labourer, sister-in-law Rose, 22, and niece Catherine, 1.

In 1881, James McGhee, 53, a coal mine labourer, resided at New Signs, Causewayside Street, Tollcross, with wife Jane, 44, children James, 21, John, 20, Edward, 18, all coal miners, Mary, 17, Bridget, 14, both factory workers, Thomas, 13, Margaret, 12, Catherine, 9, Jane, 7, Francis, 5, all at school, and Patrick, 2. James McGhee, a coal miner, was dead by 1888, however, his wife Jane McGhee nee Lafferty was still alive by then.

Mark's paternal great-great-grandparents – Felix Gunn and Mary McCabe

Mark's other paternal great-great-grandfather Felix Gunn and great-great-grandmother Mary McCabe were born around 1830, most likely in Ireland. Felix Gunn, a furnaceman, married Mary McCabe and they had a daughter Rose Ann (b. ~1864) who was born in Shotts, Lanarkshire. Felix Gunn, a furnaceman, and his wife Mary Gunn nee McCabe were still alive in 1888.

Chapter 10:

Eric Black (inside left)
Honours as an Aberdeen player:
1 European Cup Winners Cup
1 European Super Cup
2 Scottish League titles
3 Scottish Cups
1 Scottish League Cup

The young Eric Black

John Eric Black aka Eric was born on 1 October 1963 at the Maternity Hospital, Bellshill, Lanarkshire to his father Eric Black, an engineer fitter, and his mother Margaret Bogle Bingham. The birth was registered by his father Eric Black on 12 October 1963 at the Bellshill Registry Office. He is a Scottish former professional football player and coach. Black played as a striker for Aberdeen and French club Metz, and winning major trophies with both clubs. He earned two international caps for the Scotland national team. Black was forced to retire from playing at a relatively early age and became a coach, managing Motherwell and Coventry City.

Born in Bellshill when the family resided at 30 Alexander Street, Coatbridge, Black spent his early life in the Glasgow area. Then his family moved north to Nigg in the Highland region, due to his father's offshore oil job at the outset of the North Sea oil boom. He was a Scottish former professional football player and coach. He signed for Aberdeen in 1980, a week after teammate Bryan Gunn, who came from the same part of the country. Black was heavily involved in the most successful era of Aberdeen's history under Alex Ferguson. The pinnacle was their European Cup Winners' Cup victory in 1983 with a 2–1 win over Real Madrid in Gothenburg, where the 19-year-old Black scored the first goal.

Despite not being particularly tall at only 5 feet 8 inches, Black's main assets were his strength in the air and his goal scoring instincts. In February 1983, Black scored a rare hat-trick in a 3–1 win against Celtic at Parkhead. He made 180 appearances, 30 as a substitute, in all competitions for Aberdeen and scored 70 goals between 1981 and 1986. He won two Scottish League titles, three Scottish Cups and a Scottish League Cup. He also won the European Cup Winners' Cup and the European Super Cup in 1983. He missed out on a potential fourth Scottish Cup medal when Ferguson overlooked him for the 1986 final having already agreed to move abroad.

In the summer of 1986, Black transferred to Metz in France, where he continued to have a successful career. Black played as a striker for Aberdeen and French club Metz, winning major trophies with both clubs, and earned two international caps for the Scotland national team. He was forced to retire from playing at a relatively early age and became a coach, working as a manager at Motherwell and Coventry City.

Eric's parents – Eric Black and Margaret Bogle Bingham

On the day Hitler met the Japanese ambassador at the Berghof to inform him that he would invade the Soviet Union, Eric's father Eric Black was born on 3 June 1941, during WWII, at 1 Grace Avenue, Bargeddie, Lanarkshire, to father John Black, a coal miner hewer, and mother Helen Martin Grant. His father John Black registered his birth on 23 June 1941 at the Baillieston Registry Office. On the day that allied ships docked in Tobruk during the North Africa campaign, Eric's mother Margaret Bogle Bingham was born on 27 January 1941, during WWII, at 3B East Miller Street, Coatbridge, to her father Peter Drysdale Bingham, an engineer's machinist, and mother Margaret Swan Dalziel Frame. Her father Peter Bingham registered her birth on 3 February 1941 at the Coatbridge Registry Office.

Eric Black, 20, an engineer fitter, of 1 Grace Avenue, Bargeddie, married Margaret Bogle Bingham, 21, a shorthand typist, of 23 Cuparhead Avenue, Coatbridge, on 3 March 1962 at Old Monkland Church according to Church of Scotland. The wedding was conducted by Rev Walter Johnstone, minister at Old Monkland Church; the best man was Robert Black, Eric's brother, and the bridesmaid was Mary Bingham, Margaret's sister. Son John Eric Black aka Eric was born on 1 October 1963 at the Maternity Hospital, Bellshill, Lanarkshire, to father Eric Black, an engineer fitter, and his mother Margaret Bogle Bingham. The birth was registered by his father Eric Black, of 1 Grace Avenue, Bargeddie, on 12 October 1963 at the Bellshill Registry Office. Eric and Margaret later moved to the north-east of Scotland, where Eric worked in the burgeoning offshore oil industry during the North Sea oil boom of the 1970s.

Eric's paternal grandparents – John Black and Helen Martin Grant

Eric's paternal grandfather John Black was actually born illegitimately as Ebenezer Macdonald on 10 July 1904 in the Rottenrow Maternity Hospital, Glasgow, to his mother Mary Bella Macdonald, a laundress, of 368 Renfrew Street, Garnethill, Glasgow. The birth was registered by his mother M B Macdonald on 3 August 1904 at the Glasgow Registry Office.

Unable to keep baby Ebenezer, his mother Mary put him up for adoption. At that time, this was a fairly informal affair, usually run by Parish Councils, churches and various charities. Ebenezer was adopted by his stepfather John Black, a labourer, and his stepmother Matilda Graham. In 1911, Ebenezer Macdonald, 6, at school, resided at 3 Quarry Row, Gartsherrie, Coatbridge, with his stepfather John Black, 50, a brickwork labourer in the blast furnaces, stepmother Matilda, 37, and adopted stepsister Agnes Muirhead.

In 1921, Ebenezer Macdonald, 16, a railway porter with the Caledonian Railway Company, resided at 15 Gartgill Square, Gartsherrie, Old Monkland, with his stepfather John Black, 59, a general labourer with the Caledonian Railway Company, stepmother Matilda, 47, a household domestic, his adopted stepsister Agnes Muirhead, 14, a scholar, and his adopted stepbrother Robert Robertson, 2. However, Ebenezer preferred to be known by his stepfather's name, John Black.

Eric's paternal grandmother Helen Martin Grant was born on 3 August 1910 at 180f Buchanan Street, Coatbridge, Old Monkland, to father William Grant, a coal miner, and mother Isabella Augustine Totten. John Black, 24, a coal miner, married Helen Grant, 18, a domestic servant, both of 59 Gartgill Square, Coatbridge, on 8 September 1928 at 21 Hope Street, Glasgow, in a civil ceremony by warrant of the Sheriff Substitute of Lanarkshire. The witnesses were Thomas Jordan and Mary Jordan, of 5 Eastbank, Glenboig.

John and Helen had two known sons in Bargeddie; William and Eric. Son Eric Black was born on 3 June 1941, during WWII, at 1 Grace Avenue, Bargeddie, Lanarkshire, to father John Black, a coal miner hewer, and mother Helen Martin Grant. His father John Black registered his birth on 23 June 1941 at the Baillieston Registry Office. John Black, a coal miner, and his wife Helen were both still living in Bargeddie in 1962. On 3 December 1976, Ebenezer Macdonald legally changed his name to John Black in a Register of Corrected Entries (Ref: 2046/1976/GLW), which was annotated on his birth lines at General Register House, Edinburgh. This probably coincided with the death of his wife Helen Martin Black nee Grant, 66, in 1976 as registered in Baillieston, Old Monkland. A few months after Aberdeen's historic win in Gothenburg, John Black, 79, a widowed retired coal miner, still living at 1 Grace Avenue, Bargeddie, died on 30 October 1983 in Monklands District General Hospital of bronchopneumonia and gastric carcinoma as certified by Dr P A Moultrie. The death was registered by his son William Black, of 6 Cairn Drive, Linwood, on 31 October 1983 at Baillieston Registry Office.

Eric's maternal grandparents – Peter Drysdale Bingham and Margaret Swan Dalziel Frame

Eric's maternal grandfather Peter Drysdale (or Dryfesdale) Bingham was born in 1907 in Coatbridge,

Old Monkland, to father Alexander Bingham, a coal miner, and mother Margaret Bogle. Peter's father Alexander died in 1920 and in 1921, Peter, 14, an engineering labourer with William Barr & Co. construction engineers, resided at 190c Whifflet Street, Coatbridge, with his mother Margaret Bingham, 52, a widowed household domestic, and his siblings. Eric's grandmother Margaret Swan Dalziel Frame was born in 1912 in Airdrie, New Monkland to father Robert Frame, a tube worker, and mother Elizabeth Dalziel.

Peter Drysdale Bingham, 24, an engineering work machinist, of 114 Whifflet Street, Airdrie, married Margaret Swan Dalziel Frame, 18, a paper mill worker, of 118 Clark Street, Airdrie, on 15 July 1931 at the Orange Hall, Baillie's Lane, Airdrie, according to the Congregational Church. The wedding was conducted by Rev David W Thomson, Congregational minister, 32 Woodburn Avenue, Airdrie; the best man was Stewart Bingham, Peter's brother, and bridesmaid was Margaret S Watchman.

Daughter Margaret Bogle Bingham was born on 27 January 1941, during WWII, at 3b East Miller Street, Coatbridge, to father Peter Drysdale Bingham, an engineer's machinist, and mother Margaret Swan Dalziel Frame. Her father Peter Bingham registered her birth on 3 February 1941 at the Coatbridge Registry Office. Peter Drysdale Bingham, by then an iron works manager, and his wife Margaret were both alive in 1962.

Eric's paternal great-grandmother – Mary Bella MacDonald

Eric's paternal great-grandmother Mary Bella Macdonald is a bit of an enigma. She has left virtually no trail of herself in Scottish records. It is possible that Mary Bella Macdonald was born around the 1870-80s in the Highlands of Scotland, possibly Caithness or Ross-shire. In the early 1900s she came to Glasgow seeking work. Mary Bella was a laundress and lived in the city centre district of Garnethill. Son Ebenezer Macdonald was born illegitimately on 10 July 1904 in the Rottenrow Maternity Hospital, Glasgow, to mother Mary Bella Macdonald, a laundress, of 368 Renfrew Street, Garnethill, Glasgow. The birth was registered by his mother M B Macdonald on 3 August 1904 at the Glasgow Registry Office. The tenement at 368 Renfrew Street was demolished in the late 1960s as part of the construction of the M8 motorway which goes through the Charing Cross area of Glasgow.

Mary's signature was neat and legible, suggesting she had been well educated. The father of repute remained unnamed, although there is a distinct possibility his first name was Ebenezer, as this was a common practice for woman to shame the errant father. Unable to keep baby Ebenezer, Mary put him up for adoption. At that time this was an informal affair, usually run by

Parish Councils, churches and charities. However, no record has been found within the Glasgow Adoption Records, nor did Mary appear to apply to the Glasgow Poor Roll for poor relief. It is unclear what happened to Mary. However, she may have emigrated to the United States. There are unconfirmed records of women recorded as Mary B Macdonald, born in Scotland, recorded on the United States Passenger Lists heading for America in 1905 and 1907, shortly after Ebenezer was born.

Eric's paternal great-grandparents – William Grant and Isabella Augustine Totten

Eric's paternal great-grandfather William Grant was born on 15 March 1886 at 210 Gartsherrie, Old Monkland to father John Grant, an engine driver, and mother Ellen Martin. His father John Grant registered the birth on 30 March 1886 at the Coatbridge Registry Office. Eric's great-grandmother Isabella Augustine Totten, aka Bella, was born on 8 August 1890 at Ash Bank, Glenboig, New Monkland to father David Totten, a labourer, and mother Marion Gray. Her father David Totten registered the birth, signing with his 'x' mark, on 25 August 1890 at New Monkland Registry Office.

William Grant, 22, a coal miner, married Bella A Totten, 18, an outdoor worker, both of 9 Eastbank, Glenboig by Airdrie, on 24 April 1908 at home according to the United Free Church of Scotland. The wedding was conducted by Rev David Galbraith; the best man was Joseph Bell and bridesmaid was Marion Totten, Bella's sister. William and Isabella had 6 known children in Coatbridge; Marion (b. ~1909), Helen Martin (b. 3 August 1910), Mary (b. ~1911), Isabella (b. ~1915), John (b. ~1918) and Barbara (b. ~1920). Their daughter Helen Martin Grant was born on 3 August 1910 at 180f Buchanan Street, Coatbridge, Old Monkland, to father William Grant, a coal miner, and her mother Isabella Augustine Totten. In 1921, William Grant, 35, a coal miner hewer, with William Baird, Gartsherrie coal masters, resided at 59 Gartgill Square, Gartsherrie, Old Monkland, with his wife Isabella, 30, a household domestic, and children Marion, 12, Helen, 10, Mary, 8, Isabella, 6, all scholars, John, 3, and Barbara, 5 months old. William also had two boarders; Brooklyn-born American Alexander Walker, 29, a coal miner hewer with William Baird's, and wife Aberdonian-born Margaret Walker, 28, a household domestic.

At that time, Baird's were one of the largest single employers in Scotland with their vast holdings in coal mining and iron and steel. The Baird family were conservatively religious and the firm tended to employ predominantly Protestant workers, which nowadays, would have been regarded as discriminatory. William Grant, a labourer, and wife Isabella were both alive in Coatbridge in 1928.

Eric's maternal great-grandparents – Alexander Bingham and Margaret Bogle

Eric's maternal great-grandfather Alexander Bingham was born around 1868 in Old Monkland to a father surnamed Bingham and his mother surnamed Cochrane. Eric's great-grandmother Margaret Bogle was born around 1869 in Glasgow, Lanarkshire. Alexander Bingham, a coal miner, married Margaret Bogle in 1888 in Coatbridge, Old Monkland. Alexander and wife Margaret had 4 known children in Whifflet, Old Monkland; Archibald (b. ~1897), Margaret (b. ~1905), Peter (b. 1907) and Stewart (b. ~1910). Their son was Peter Drysdale (or Dryfesdale) Bingham born in 1907 in Coatbridge, Old Monkland, to father Alexander Bingham, a coal miner, and mother Margaret Bogle. Alexander Bingham, a coal miner, 52, died in 1920 in Coatbridge.

The following year, in 1921, Margaret Bingham, 52, a widowed household domestic, resided at 190c Whifflet Street, Coatbridge, with children Archibald, 24, a blacksmith with Merry & Cunningham pig iron manufacturers, Margaret, 16, a household domestic, Peter, 14, an engineering labourer with William Barr & Co. construction engineers, Stewart, 11, a scholar, and a boarder Robert Magilton, 23, a coal miner hewer with Barr & Higgins coal masters. Margaret Bingham nee Bogle was dead by 1931.

Eric's maternal great-grandparents – Robert Frame and Elizabeth Dalziel

Eric's paternal great-grandfather Robert Frame and his great-grandmother Elizabeth Dalziel were born around 1885 in New Monkland, Lanarkshire. Robert Frame, a tube worker, married Elizabeth Frame in 1911 in Airdrie, New Monkland. Daughter Margaret Swan Dalziel Frame was born in 1912 in Airdrie, New Monkland, to her father Robert Frame, a tube worker, and mother Elizabeth Dalziel. Robert Frame, a tube worker, and wife Elizabeth were still alive in 1931 in Airdrie.

Chapter 11:

Peter Weir (outside left)
Honours as an Aberdeen player:
1 European Cup Winners Cup
2 Scottish League titles
3 Scottish Cups

The young Peter Weir

Peter Russell Weir was born on 18 January 1958 at the Maternity Hospital, Johnstone, Renfrewshire to father Archibald Russell Weir, an airline accountant, and mother Mary Caldwell Milne. His father A R Weir registered the birth on 1 February 1958 at the Johnstone Registry Office. At the time the family lived at Kirkhill Cottage, Neilston Road, Neilston. Weir is a Scottish former footballer, best known for his time with Aberdeen, playing as an outside winger.

PRIDE OF THE DONS

Having been a supporter of Aberdeen as a boy, Weir joined the club from St Mirren in 1981 for £300,000 plus Ian Scanlon, which was then a club record. Alex McLeish, who had attended Barrhead High School and played in youth teams alongside Weir, was already playing at Aberdeen. Weir had been brought to St Mirren from Neilston Juniors in 1978 by Alex Ferguson, who was acrimoniously sacked by the Paisley club within days of Weir's arrival. Ferguson was soon appointed as manager of Aberdeen, following the departure of Billy McNeill to Celtic. He then successfully sought to make his former signing Weir part of the new Dons setup.

Weir made 237 appearances and scored 38 goals whilst at Pittodrie, and was capped by Scotland on six occasions. He won two Scottish League titles and three Scottish Cups, as well as the European Cup Winners' Cup in 1983, playing a crucial role in the final. Deep into extra time, Weir placed a slide-rule pass to Mark McGhee, whose pinpoint cross was headed in by John Hewitt to beat Real Madrid 2-1. In December 1987, Weir left the Dons to move across the border to sign for Leicester City for £80,000. Upon leaving Leicester in 1989, he returned to St Mirren and later played for Ayr United. Weir retired from playing in 1992.

Peter's parents – Archibald Russell Weir and Mary Caldwell Milne

Peter's father Archibald Russell Weir was born on 9 September 1929 at 18 Millview Terrace, Neilston, to father Peter Weir, a railway clerk, and mother Mary McKay Harrison. His father Peter Weir registered the birth on 18 September 1929 at Neilston Registry Office. At the time, the family lived at 17 Langside Avenue, Viewpark, Uddingston. Peter's mother Mary Caldwell Milne was born around 1932 in Glasgow to her father William Milne, a chemical dispenser, and her mother Margaret Caldwell. Archibald Russell Weir, 23, an aero-engineer's costing clerk, of 114 Chirnside Road, Cardonald, Glasgow, married Mary Caldwell Milne, 21, a shorthand typist, of 121 Ladykirk Drive, Cardonald, Glasgow, on 17 January 1953 in a civil ceremony at the Blythswood Registry Office, Glasgow. The wedding was conducted by W G Donaldson, registrar; the best man was Robert L Brown and the bridesmaid was Isabella G Fryer. Son Peter Russell Weir was born on 18 January 1958 at the Maternity Hospital, Johnstone, Renfrewshire to father Archibald Russell Weir, an airline accountant, and mother Mary Caldwell Milne. His father A R Weir registered the birth on 1 February 1958 at the Johnstone Registry Office. At the time the family lived at Kirkhill Cottage, Neilston.

On 3 March 1982, the year before his son Peter lifted the ECWC in Gothenburg, Archie, of 4 Lochlibo Crecent, Barrhead, had the sad duty of registering the death of his father Peter Weir, 79, a retired District Traffic Manager, at the Glengarnock Registry Office.

Peter's paternal grandparents – Peter Weir and Mary McKay Harrison

Peter's paternal grandfather Peter Weir was born on 21 June 1902 in Stoneyburn Cottage, Whitburn, Linlithgowshire (now the county of West Lothian), to his father Archibald Russell Weir, a railway signalman, and mother Janet Smith Lind. His father Archibald R Weir registered the birth on 5 July 1902 at Whitburn Registry Office. After leaving school Peter got a job in the rail industry and by 1923 during the amalgamation of the 'Big Four', Peter was transferred to the London Midland & Scottish Railway Company (LMS). Peter's paternal grandmother Mary McKay Harrison, aka May, was born around 1906 possibly in Neilston, Renfrewshire to father William Harrison, a packing case maker, and mother Janet McDonald. After leaving school May got a job as a thread-mill machinist, almost certainly with the local R F & J Alexander's Crofthead Mill which exported threads worldwide.

Peter Weir, 26, a railway clerk, of Springbank, Neilston Road, Neilston, married wife Mary McKay Harrison, 23, a thread-mill machinist, of 18 Millview Terrace, Neilston, on 17 May 1929 at the famous Ca

D'Oro Building in Union Street, Glasgow according to Church of Scotland. The wedding was conducted by Rev Robert Barr, minister of Neilston; the best man was James Lind Weir, Peter's brother, and the bridesmaid was Christina McP Brown. Son Archibald Russell Weir was born on 9 September 1929 at 18 Millview Terrace, Neilston to his father Peter Weir, a railway clerk, and mother Mary McKay Harrison. His father Peter Weir registered the birth on 18 September 1929 at Neilston Registry Office. At the time, the family lived at 17 Langside Avenue, Viewpark, Uddingston.

Peter Weir, a railway relief stationmaster working for British Railways, and his wife May were living in Glasgow in 1953. Peter Weir, 79, a retired BR District Traffic Manager, was found dead about 19.00 hours on 1 March 1982 outside his home at 60 Kirkland Road, Glengarnock. Peter died of left ventricular failure, hypertensive heart disease and cirrhosis of the liver as certified by Dr William Wallace. The death was registered by his son A R Weir, of 4 Lochlibo Crescent, Barrhead, on 3 March 1982 at the Glengarnock Registry Office. His wife Mary McKay Weir nee Harrison was still alive in 1982.

Peter's paternal great-grandparents – Archibald Russell Weir and Janet Smith Lind

Peter's paternal great-grandfather Archibald Russell Weir was born on 8 June 1874 at Uphall, Linlithgowshire to father Peter Weir, a labourer, and mother Margaret Russell. The birth was registered by his father Peter Weir on 20 June 1874 at Broxburn Registry Office. After leaving school, Archibald got a job as a pointsman with the Caledonian Railway Company. Peter's great-grandmother Janet Smith Lind was born around 1875 in West Calder, Midlothian to father James Lind, a railway platelayer, and mother Marion Wright. It seems likely that Archie, whose grandmother was Helen Lind, and Janet were cousins. In 1901, Archibald R Weir, 26, a pointsman, resided at Bents Station, Whitburn.

Archibald Russell Weir, 27, a railway signalman, of Bents Cottage, Fauldhouse, Whitburn, married Janet Smith Lind, 26, a domestic servant, of Harburn, West Calder, on 21 June 1901 at the Maitland Hotel, 29-37 Shandwick Place, Edinburgh according to the United Free Church. The wedding was conducted by the Rev Robert James Drummond; the best man was Robert Weir, Archie's brother, and the best maid was Marion Lind, Janet's sister. Bents Cottage, a railway building beside Bents Station, was on the Wilsontown, Morningside & Coltness Branch of the Caledonian Railway. The Maitland Hotel, designed in 1876 by McGibbon & Ross, now retail outlets, is a Category C listed building in Edinburgh on British Listed Buildings. Archie and Janet had 6 known children; in Whitburn, Peter (b. 21 June 1902), James Lind (b. ~1904), in Avondale, Marion Wright Lind (b. ~1906), Margaret Russell Lind (b. ~1910), Norman A (b. ~1912) and in Applegarth, Robert (b. ~1917).

Son Peter Weir was born on 21 June 1902 in Stoneyburn Cottage, Whitburn, Linlithgowshire to his father Archibald Russell Weir, a railway signalman, and his mother Janet Smith Lind. His father Archibald R Weir registered the birth on 5 July 1902 at Whitburn Registry Office. Around 1906, the Weir family moved to Avondale.

In 1911, Archibald R Weir, 38, a stationmaster on the Caledonian Railway, resided at Ryeland Station, Avondale, Lanarkshire, with wife Janet L, 38, children Peter, 8, James L, 7, both at school, Marion W L, 5, and Margaret R L, 7 months old. Also visiting Archie's home was Mary McCleary, 57, a widow, to see her lodger son William G McCleary, 29, a creamery manager. Ryeland Station was on the short-lived Darvel and Strathaven Branch (1905-39), jointly run by the Glasgow & South Western Railway and Caledonian Railway. Around 1917, during WW1, the family moved to Applegarth in Dumfriesshire.

In 1921, Archibald R Weir, 47, a stationmaster with the Caledonian Railway, resided at Dinwoodie Station, Applegarth, with wife Janet L, 46, a housewife domestic, children Marion, 15, Margaret, 10, Norman A, 9, all at school, and Robert, 4. Dinwoodie Station lay on the West Coast Main Line, 6 miles north of Lockerbie. In 1923, Archie was transferred as part of the 'Big Four' amalgamation to the London Midland & Scottish Railway Company.

On 25 October 1928 a fatal accident took place near Dinwoodie due to signaller error. Four people were killed and five injured. The two drivers and two firemen died instantly when their double-headed passenger express, the Royal Highlander, collided with a broken-down freight train. Archibald Russell Weir, a stationmaster with the LMS, and his wife Janet Weir nee Lind were living at Springbank, Station Brae, Neilston in 1929.

Peter's paternal great-great-grandparents – Peter Weir and Margaret Russell

Peter's paternal great-great-grandfather Peter Weir was born around 1835 probably in Midlothian to father Robert Weir, a gardener, and mother Helen Lind, who may have been related to Janet Smith Lind, given the rarity of the surname, which tends to be of Olde Germanic origin. Peter's great-great-grandmother Margaret Russell was born about 1833 probably in Linlithgowshire to father Archibald Russell, a farmer, and mother Elizabeth Smith. Peter Weir, 27, a farm servant, of Muirhousedykes, West Calder, married Margaret Russell, 29, a farmer's daughter, of Stoneheap Farm, Whitburn, on 9 December 1862 at Margaret's home according to the Free Church of Scotland. The wedding was conducted by Rev David Herdwick, minister of Longridge Free Church; the witnesses were John Cunningham and James Lind.

James Lind was probably Janet Smith Lind's father and Helen Lind's brother. In the late 19th century, Stoneheap at Bents Station became heavily associated with the Scottish Shale Oil Company and Peter went on to become a shale pit work labourer. Peter and wife Margaret had 2 known sons; Archibald and Robert. Son Archibald Russell Weir was born on 8 June 1874 at Uphall, Linlithgowshire to father Peter Weir, a labourer, and mother Margaret Russell. The birth was registered by his father Peter Weir on 20 June 1874 at the Broxburn Registry Office. Peter Weir, a pit work labourer, and his wife Margaret were both still alive in 1901 at Bents Cottage, Whitburn.

Part 2:

The other Gothenburg players 1983

Campaign medallists

Chapter 12:

Stuart Kennedy (right back)

Honours as an Aberdeen player:
1 European Cup Winners Cup
1 Scottish League title
1 Scottish Cup
1 Scottish League Cup

The young Stuart Kennedy

Stuart Robert Kennedy was born on 31 May 1953 in Grangemouth, Stirlingshire. He is a Scottish former footballer who played as a right-back for Falkirk and Aberdeen. He made eight appearances for the Scotland national team. Kennedy was raised in Grangemouth, starting out as an amateur with Bothkennar YM and made 101 appearances for Falkirk from 1971 to 1976.

PRIDE OF THE DONS

He moved to Aberdeen in 1976 for £30,000 and featured prominently in Aberdeen's greatest period of success. A hard-working, skillful player, he won every major domestic honour in his time at Pittodrie, namely the Scottish League title in 1979–80, the Scottish Cup in 1981–82, and the 1976–77 Scottish League Cup. During the second leg 3–2 victory over the mighty German side Bayern Munich in the European Cup Winners' Cup semi-final in 1983, Kennedy picked up a serious knee injury after catching his studs at the edge of the pitch. Having played in every game of Aberdeen's European campaign up to then, he was forced to watch from the dugout when his colleagues faced Real Madrid in the final in Gothenburg, Sweden. The Dons lifted the trophy after a 2–1 victory over the Spanish giants. Kennedy earned himself a place on the substitutes' bench, despite being unable to play, thanks to an act of respect from his coach Alex Ferguson. The injury proved so serious that Kennedy never played professionally again.

Stuart Robert Kennedy's family history has not been researched for this book.

Chapter 13:

Bryan Gunn (goalkeeper)
Honours as an Aberdeen player:
1 European Cup Winners' Cup
1 Scottish League Cup

The young Bryan Gunn

Bryan James Gunn was born on 22 December 1963 in Dunbar Hospital, Thurso, Caithness, "twenty miles from John O'Groats". Gunn's father was James William Donald Gunn, an oil rigger, and his mother was Jessie Sinclair, working as a canteen worker at Dounreay nuclear power plant. At the time, the family lived at 2 New Houses, Weydale, Thurso. The birth was registered by his father J Gunn on 10 January 1964 at the Thurso Registry Office. Gunn's parents had married despite being on opposite sides of a reputed family feud stretching back to the 16th century.

The Gunn family home in Weydale, Thurso was a farm and the young Bryan would often pester the farmhands to play football with him. They would use a turnip if no ball was available. From the age of four he was keen on goalkeeping; he was fearless of injury and enjoyed diving on the ball. When Gunn was four-and-a-half, the family moved south to Invergordon, 20 miles from Inverness. He attended Park Primary School and joined the school football team. Future professional Bobby Geddes, who went on to play for Dundee, was favoured over him as first-choice goalkeeper for the team; Gunn played as an outfield player until Geddes moved on to secondary school.

Gunn attended secondary school at Invergordon Academy from 1975 to 1980. At the age of 13, he was invited to play for the under-15 Invergordon FC team. The team was beaten 9–0 in Gunn's debut, but his subsequent performances attracted the attention of national selectors, and he joined the Scotland under-15 squad around the same time as he signed for Aberdeen at age 14. He commenced his professional career with Aberdeen in 1980, signing a week prior to Eric Black who came from the same part of the country, and he forged a good relationship with manager Alex Ferguson.

As a youngster, Gunn did not always play in goal and he was viewed as a handy outfield player in his early years at Aberdeen. Ferguson recalled, "He could strike a ball as well as anyone, so well in fact that I once played him at centre-forward in a reserve match...He scored a brilliant goal...It was a marvellous moment." However, as a professional and at his adult height of 6 foot 2 inches, Gunn settled into playing in goal. Gunn ascribed much of his goalkeeping success to the support of Belgian Marc De Clerck, a specialist goalkeeping coach at Aberdeen. At a time when few British teams provided such training, De Clerck introduced Gunn and Jim Leighton to what were then innovative training techniques. Gunn also noted the influence of Aberdeen coach Teddy Scott, who taught the value of hard work and dedication. Gunn's training and performances for the reserve team and an occasional first-team appearance paid dividends. He was called up for the Scotland under-21 team, and made his debut in November 1983 against East Germany. He won Scottish League Cup and European Cup Winners' Cup medals with Aberdeen, although he was an unused substitute in both finals.

He made an unexpected appearance in the 1986 European Cup quarter final, against Gothenburg, because Jim Leighton had lost his contact lenses. As Leighton was unlikely to be dislodged, Ferguson promised to find Gunn another club, and fulfilled his pledge when he sold him for £100,000 to Norwich City in October 1986. Gunn spent 12 successful years at Carrow Road, before joining Hibernian for a short spell in 1998–99.

Bryan Gunn's son Angus Fraser James Gunn, born on 22 January 1996 in Norwich, and he followed his father as a professional goalkeeper and plays for Norwich City. He played at England under-21 level under Gareth Southgate, but in March 2023 he declared for Steve Clarke's Scotland national team. He played in the European Championship qualifiers, beginning with five consecutive victories over Cyprus (twice), Spain, then Norway and Georgia, in which Gunn made a significant contribution. At the time of writing, although suffering a return defeat to Spain in Seville, Scotland qualified for the 2024 UEFA Championship finals in Germany. Gunn played in Germany, however, Scotland failed to reach the knock-out stages, taking only one point from three games.

Bryan's parents – James William Donald Gunn and Jessie Sinclair

Bryan's father James William Donald Gunn was born on 30 August 1936 in Sibster, Halkirk, Caithness to father James William Gunn, a farmer, and mother Mary Ann Sutherland. The birth was registered by his father James W Gunn on 8 September 1936 at Halkirk Registry Office. His mother Jessie Sinclair was born around 1939 in Weydale, Thurso to father Herbert Sinclair, a lorry driver, and mother Helen Elliot Munro.

As a young man James was a keen amateur sportsman, playing football on the right wing for local team Invergordon FC and winning medals at highland games events. James William Donald Gunn, 24, a farm worker, of Sibmister Farm, Castletown, married Jessie Sinclair, 21, a housemaid, of 4 New Houses, Weydale, Thurso, on 21 October 1960 at Olrig Church, Castletown according to the Church of Scotland. The wedding was conducted by D Nairn McLeish, minister of Olrig Church; the witnesses were relatives H Sinclair and H Gunn. By family repute, this marriage brought to an end a centuries-old feud between the Gunn and Sinclair families.

James worked as a long-distance lorry driver, but by 1963 he was a rigger in the newly developing North Sea oil industry. Son Bryan James Gunn was born on 22 December 1963 in Dunbar Hospital, Thurso to his father James William Donald Gunn, an oil rigger, and his mother Jessie Sinclair, a canteen worker at the now decommissioned Dounreay nuclear power plant, and the family lived at 2 New Houses, Weydale, Thurso. The birth was registered by his father J Gunn on 10 January 1964 at the Thurso Registry Office. In 1968, when Bryan was four-and-a-half, the family moved south to live in Invergordon, 20 miles north of Inverness, so that James could be closer to the ever-expanding oil industry.

Bryan's paternal grandparents – James William Gunn and Mary Ann Mitchell Coghill Sutherland

Bryan's paternal grandfather James William Gunn was born on 9 April 1911 in Thrumster, Wick to father William Swanson Gunn, a police constable, and mother Maggie Duncan Morgan. The birth was registered by his father William S Gunn on 1 May 1911 at the Wick Registry Office. Bryan's grandmother Mary Ann Mitchell Coghill Sutherland was born illegitimately on 21 October 1914, during the first weeks of WWI at Shuster, Wick to mother Elizabeth Sutherland, a domestic servant. The birth was registered by mother Elizabeth Sutherland on 11 November 1914 at Wick Registry Office. The inclusion of middle names Mitchell and Coghill are likely to be Elizabeth's way of shaming the errant father, as this was common practice at that time.

In 1936, James was working as a farm servant at Hoy; the area is famous for its vertical sea stack, the Old Man of Hoy, a challenging climb for even the most experienced climbers. James William Gunn, 25, a farm servant, of Hoy, Thurso, married Mary Ann Mitchell Coghill Sutherland, 21, a domestic servant, of Sibster, Halkirk, on 19 June 1936 at the Manse, Halkirk according to the Church of Scotland forms. The wedding was conducted by Rev John MacInnes, minister of Halkirk; the best man was Donald Gunn, of Camilla Street, Halkirk, and the best maid was Mary Bruce, of Stirkoke Farm. Ten weeks later, son James William Donald Gunn was born on 30 August 1936 in Sibster, Halkirk, Caithness to father James William Gunn, a farmer, and mother Mary Ann Sutherland. The birth was registered by his father James W Gunn on 8 September 1936 at Halkirk Registry Office. James, a farm worker, and Mary Ann were both still alive in 1960 in Castletown.

Bryan's paternal great-grandparents – William Swanson Gunn and Maggie Duncan Morgan

Bryan's paternal great-grandfather William Swanson Gunn and great-grandmother Maggie Duncan Morgan were both born around 1880 in Caithness. William and Maggie had a son James William Gunn born on 9 April 1911 in Thrumster, Wick to father William Swanson Gunn, a police constable, and mother Maggie Duncan Morgan. The birth was registered by his father William S Gunn on 1 May 1911 at Wick Registry Office. Following WWI, William became a farmer at Hoy, Thurso. William Swanson Gunn, a farmer at Hoy, was still alive in 1936, however, his wife Maggie was deceased by then.

Chapter 14:

Andy Watson (midfielder)
Honours as an Aberdeen player:
1 European Cup Winners Cup
1 Scottish League title
1 Scottish Cup

The young Andy Watson

Andrew Watson, aka Andy, was born on 3 September 1959 in Fonthill Maternity Home, 62 Fonthill Road, Ferryhill, Aberdeen to father Dennis Watson, a textile worker, and mother May Ingram. The birth was registered by father Dennis Watson on 21 September 1959 at the Aberdeen Registry Office. At the time the family were living at 52 Manor Avenue, Aberdeen.

DEREK NIVEN

He is a Scottish former professional footballer and coach. During his playing career, Watson had spells at Aberdeen, Leeds United, then Heart of Midlothian and Hibernian. As a coach, he worked with clubs in Scotland and England, and has been part of the Scottish national team management setup in two separate spells. Scouted at Sunnyside Boys Club, he began his professional career in 1976 with hometown club Aberdeen having been signed by Ally MacLeod, however, it was under manager Alex Ferguson that saw his career blossom. Watson was a winner of the 1979–80 Scottish League title and the 1982–83 Scottish Cup, and he was also an unused substitute in the 1983 European Cup Winners' Cup Final victory over Real Madrid in rain-soaked Gothenburg. However, he was never a regular starter in such a strong Dons team and left the club at the end of that season. Watson had spells with Leeds United 1983–84 under Eddie Gray, Hearts 1984–87 under Alex MacDonald and Sandy Jardine, and Hibernian 1987–89 under Alex Miller. Watson then went into coaching at club and international level with Scotland.

Andy's parents – Dennis Watson and May Ingram

Andy's father Dennis Watson was born on 2 July 1938 at 23 Canal Terrace, Woodside, Aberdeen to father Francis Shearer Watson, a general carter, and mother Annabella Young, previously married as Davidson.

PRIDE OF THE DONS

The birth was registered by mother Annabella Watson on 23 July 1938 at the Aberdeen Registry Office. This was about midway through the Spanish Civil War, seen as a precursor to WWII, in which both Fascists Hitler and Mussolini employed their air forces to assist Franco's Nationalist army towards ultimate victory. However, Franco did not repay the two Fascist dictators, as he kept Spain neutral during WWII.

Andy's mother Mary Ingram aka May was born around 1941, during WWII, in Aberdeen to her father Alexander Forbes Ingram, a builder's labourer, and mother Adeline Willis. Dennis Watson, 20, a coal merchant's lorry driver, of 52 Manor Avenue, Aberdeen, married May Ingram, 18, a butcher's shop assistant, of 16 Seaton Road, Aberdeen, on 21 March 1959 at Woodside South Church of Scotland. The wedding was conducted by Rev John Stewart, minister of Woodside South; the best man was Ronald McGlashan and the best maid was Grace Thomson.

Son Andrew Watson was born on 3 September 1959 at Fonthill Maternity Home, 62 Fonthill Road in the Southern District of Aberdeen to father Dennis Watson, a textile worker, and mother May Ingram. The birth was registered by his father Dennis Watson on 21 September 1959 at the Aberdeen Registry Office.

Andy's paternal grandparents – Francis Shearer Watson and Annabella Watson previously Davidson nee Young

Andy's paternal grandfather Francis Shearer Watson was born on 25 September 1897 at 793 Great Northern Road, Woodside, Aberdeen to father Andrew Watson, a general carter, and mother Annabella Scott. The birth was registered by his father Andrew Watson on 15 October 1897 at the Woodside Registry Office. It is likely that Francis served during WWI, probably from 1916–18, although, his regiment has not been identified, as a few soldiers named Francis S Watson served in the Great War.

Andy's paternal grandmother Annabella Young aka Anna was born around 1897 in Aberdeen to father Alexander Young, a stone cutter, and mother Maggie Mitchell. Exactly a month after the Armistice in WWI, Annabella Young, 21, a wool mill worker, of 21 Canal Terrace, Woodside, Aberdeen, married her first husband Gordon Davidson, 23, a box maker, of 473 Great Northern Road, Woodside, Aberdeen, on 11 December 1918 in Woodside Church of Scotland. However, by 1926, Annabella was a widow with the death of her husband Gordon. Francis Shearer Watson, 29, a general carter, of 753 Great Northern Road, Woodside, Aberdeen, married Annabella Young Davidson, 29, a widowed wood mill worker, of 21 Canal Terrace, Woodside, Aberdeen, on Hogmanay 31 December 1926 at Woodside Parish Manse according to the Church of Scotland.

The wedding was conducted by Rev Robert Laird Sneddon, minister of Woodside; the witnesses were J Watson and J McKissock. Son Dennis Watson was born on 2 July 1938 at 23 Canal Terrace, Woodside, Aberdeen to his father Francis Shearer Watson, a general carter, and his mother Annabella Young, previously married as Davidson. The birth was registered by his mother Annabella Watson on 23 July 1938 at Aberdeen Registry Office. Francis Shearer Watson, a firewood merchant, was recorded as dead by 1959, although, his wife Annabella was still alive at that time.

Andy's maternal grandparents – Alexander Forbes Ingram and Adeline Willis

Andy's maternal grandfather Alexander Forbes Ingram was born around 1905 in Aberdeenshire and his grandmother Adeline Willis was born in 1908 in the St Nicholas parish, Aberdeen to a father surnamed Willis and mother surnamed McCallum. Alexander Forbes Ingram, 24, a builder's labourer, married wife Adeline Willis, 21, in 1929 in St Machar, Aberdeen. Daughter Mary Ingram aka May was born around 1941, during WWII, in Aberdeen to father Alexander Forbes Ingram, a builder's labourer, and her mother Adeline Willis. Alexander, a builder's labourer, and his wife Adeline were both still alive in 1959 and living at 16 Seaton Road, Aberdeen.

Chapter 15:

John Hewitt (forward)
Honours as an Aberdeen player:
1 European Cup Winners Cup
1 European Super Cup
3 Scottish League titles
4 Scottish Cups
1 Scottish League Cup

The young John Hewitt

John Hewitt was born on 9 February 1963 in Fonthill Maternity Home, 62 Fonthill Road, Aberdeen, Aberdeenshire to father John Skinner Hewitt, a joiner journeyman, and mother Winifred Mary Beattie. The birth was registered by his father John Hewitt on 21 February 1963. At the time the family were living at 204 School Drive, Seaton, Aberdeen. Hewitt is a Scottish former footballer and manager, who spend the major part of his playing career with Aberdeen, but also had spells with Celtic and St Mirren among other clubs. He also spent a short time in management in Ireland with Dundalk before retiring from the game in 1999. Hewitt is best known as the scorer of a number of significant goals for Aberdeen, including his legendary winning goal in the 1983 European Cup Winners' Cup final in Gothenburg.

Hewitt attended Cornhill Primary and played for Middlefield Wasps Boys' Club in Aberdeen. He was a schoolboy international before signing for Aberdeen, the club he had supported as a boy. He made his full debut for Aberdeen in 1979 at the age of 17 and by the 1981–82 season had become a regular in the side. In January 1982, Hewitt scored the only goal of the game in a third round Scottish Cup tie against Motherwell. This goal, timed at 9.6 seconds, was not only the fastest recorded in Scottish Cup history, but proved to be the first step in Aberdeen's stepping stone to the following season's European success. Aberdeen qualified for the European Cup Winners' Cup by going on to win the Scottish Cup that season.

The following season, Hewitt again featured prominently for Aberdeen, but it is for two substitute appearances in Europe that he is best known. On 16 March 1983, Hewitt came off the bench to score the winning goal in the Cup Winners' Cup quarter-final tie against Bayern Munich, and then repeated the feat by scoring the winner in extra time in the final against Real

Madrid. This earned him the moniker of "Super-Sub".

Hewitt also scored twice in the 1986 Scottish Cup Final against Hearts – a game in which he was named 'Man of the Match'. In all, he won three Scottish League titles, four Scottish Cup winner's medals, one Scottish League Cup winner's medal as well as the European Cup Winners' Cup and the European Super Cup while at Aberdeen. In 1989, Hewitt moved to Celtic, but failed to break into the first team on a regular basis, and subsequently spent four seasons with St Mirren from 1992–96. A short, unsuccessful spell as player-manager of Dundalk was notable only for the fact he scored the only goal of a pre-season friendly against Aberdeen. Hewitt retired from the game in 1999 after a season as assistant manager to his former Aberdeen team-mate Doug Rougvie at Cove Rangers. He was inducted into the Aberdeen "Hall of Fame" as one of the founding members in 2003.

John's parents – John Skinner Hewitt and Winifred Mary Beattie

John's father John Skinner Hewitt was born on 7 July 1931 at 6 Castle Terrace, Aberdeen to father James Hewitt, a general carter, and mother Isabella Gordon. The birth was registered by his father James Hewitt on 29 July 1931 at the Aberdeen Registry Office.

John's mother Winifred Mary Beattie was born in 1938 in Aberdeen to father Edwin Thomson Beattie, a commission agent's clerk, and mother Winifred Mary Spence. John Skinner Hewitt, 30, a joiner journeyman, of 204 School Drive, Seaton, Aberdeen, married Winifred Mary Beattie, 24, a commercial clerkess, of 341 North Anderson Drive, Aberdeen, on 5 May 1962 at Middlefield Church of Scotland. The wedding was conducted by Rev John Logie, minister of Middlefield Parish Church; the witnesses were W E Baxter and D Rae. Son John Hewitt was born on 9 February 1963 in Fonthill Maternity Home, 62 Fonthill Road, Aberdeen to father John Skinner Hewitt, a joiner journeyman, and mother Winifred Mary Beattie. The birth was registered by his father John Hewitt on 21 February 1963 at the Aberdeen Registry Office.

John's paternal grandparents – James Hewitt and Isabella Gordon

John's paternal grandfather James Hewitt was born about 1889 in Aberdeenshire to father James Hewitt, a cash collector, and mother Janet Ross. John's grandmother Isabella Gordon was born about 1890 in Aberdeenshire to father George Gordon, a stone polisher, and mother Isabella McIntosh. James Hewitt, 20, a general carter, of 37 Woolmanhill, Gilcomston, Aberdeen, married wife Isabella Gordon, 19, a fishworker, of 47 St Andrew Street, Gilcomston, Aberdeen, on Hogmanay 31 December 1908 at Isabella's home according to the Church of Scotland. The wedding was conducted by Rev George Andrew Johnston, minister of John Knox Parish Church; the best man was William Hewitt, James's brother, and the best maid was Minnie Davidson.

Son John Skinner Hewitt was born on 7 July 1931 at 6 Castle Terrace, Aberdeen to father James Hewitt, a general carter, and mother Isabella Gordon. The birth was registered by his father James Hewitt on 29 July 1931 at the Aberdeen Registry Office. James Hewitt, a retired general carter, was still alive in Aberdeen in 1962, however, his wife Isabella was dead by then.

John's maternal grandparents – Edwin Thomson Beattie and Winifred Mary Spence

John's maternal grandfather Edwin Thomson Beattie was born in 1901 in Leith North, Edinburgh, Midlothian to a father surnamed Beattie and mother surnamed Baleman. John's grandmother Winifred Mary Spence was born in 1905 in St Machar, Aberdeen to a father surnamed Spence and mother surnamed Watt. Edwin Thomson Beattie, 26, married Winifred Mary Spence, 22, in 1927 in St Machar, Aberdeen.

Daughter Winifred Mary Beattie was born in 1938 in Aberdeen to father Edwin Thomson Beattie, a commission agent's clerk, and mother Winifred Mary Spence. Edwin and Winnie were both still alive in 1962 and living at 341 North Anderson Drive, Cummings Park, Aberdeen.

Chapter 16:

Ian Angus (midfielder)

**Honours as an Aberdeen player:
1 European Cup Winners Cup**

The young Ian Angus

Ian Allan Angus was born on 19 November 1961 in a nursing home at 12 Claremont Terrace, Park, Glasgow, Lanarkshire to his father John Angus, a fishmonger, and mother Margaret Steel Rogan Miller. The birth was registered by his mother Margaret Angus on 8 December 1961 at the Glasgow Registry Office. At the time the family resided at 6 Blairgrove Place, Coatbridge, Lanarkshire. No.12 Claremont Terrace is part of a Category A Listed Building built around 1841 in the exclusive Park district of Glasgow by architect John Baird I and it is currently valued around £1 million.

Angus is a Scottish former professional footballer. As a boy he played for Eastercraigs Boys Club, a club which also produced Aberdeen stars Jim Leighton and Willie Miller. Angus started his career in 1980 at Aberdeen, playing in 84 league matches during his 7 years at Pittodrie. He was part of the Aberdeen squad who won the European Cup Winners' Cup in 1983 in Gothenburg, although, he was an unused substitute in the final against Real Madrid. Ian Allan Angus, 25, a professional footballer, married Margaret Muir McLean McInnes on 12 June 1987. That same year in 1987, Angus transferred to Dundee, which brought a similar number of appearances in only three seasons and it saw Angus transfer to Motherwell in 1990. In his first season at Fir Park, he helped Motherwell, managed by ex-Ranger Tommy McLean, on their way to a famous victory in the Scottish Cup, scoring in the 4–3 win against Dundee United, managed by Jim McLean, Tommy's brother. As the two managers were brothers it was dubbed 'The Family Final'.

In 1994, Angus left Motherwell and joined Clyde, playing in the majority of matches over the next two seasons. His finest moment as a Clyde player came when he scored the opening goal against Rangers in the Scottish Cup, although Clyde went on to lose 4–1. A spell at Albion Rovers added a few more appearances.

Angus made one League Cup appearance for Stirling Albion at the start of the 1998–99 season, when he then retired from his playing career.

Ian's parents – John Angus and Margaret Steel Rogan Miller

Ian's father John Angus was born in 1919 in Coatbridge, Old Monkland, Lanarkshire to father George Angus, a fishmonger, and his mother Agnes Forsyth Waterston. Ian's mother Margaret Steel Rogan Miller was born in 1920 in Coatbridge to father Thomas Miller, a forge manager, andher mother Margaret Steel Rogan. John Angus, 28, a fishmonger, of 6 Blairgrove Place, Coatbridge, married wife Margaret Steel Rogan Miller, 27, of 22 Mitchell Street, Kirkwood, Coatbridge on 7 April 1948 at 193 Bath Street, Glasgow, a Category A Listed Building, according to the Church of Scotland. The wedding was conducted by the Rev J Anderson, minister of Old Monkland Parish Church; the best man was Ralph M Cowan and the best maid was Isabella N Miller, Margaret's sister.

Ian Allan Angus was born on 19 November 1961 in a nursing home at 12 Claremont Terrace, Park, Glasgow, Lanarkshire to his father John Angus, a fishmonger, and mother Margaret Steel Rogan Miller. The birth was registered by his mother Margaret Angus on

8 December 1961 at the Glasgow Registry Office. At the time the family resided at 6 Blairgrove Place, Coatbridge. John Angus, a fishmonger was dead by 1987, but his wife Margaret was still alive in Coatbridge.

Ian's paternal grandparents – George Angus and Agnes Forsyth Waterston

Ian's paternal grandfather George Angus was born in 1879 in Kelvin, Glasgow to his father surnamed Angus and mother surnamed Little. At the age of 20, George Angus enlisted in the British Army and he served during the Boer War in the South Africa campaign from 1899 to 1902. Ian's paternal grandmother Agnes Forsyth Waterston was born about 1883 in Coatbridge, Old Monkland, Lanarkshire to father surnamed Waterston and mother surnamed Robb.

It is likely that George, who would have been an experienced reservist, also served in WWI, given that he did not marry until after the war. George Angus, 39, a fishmonger, married Agnes Forsyth Waterston, 37, in 1919 in Coatbridge and son John Angus was born in 1919 in Coatbridge, Old Monkland. In 1948, George and Agnes lived at 6 Blairgrove Place, Coatbridge. George Angus, 88, died in 1968 in Cadder Eastern district and his wife Agnes Forsyth Angus nee Waterston, 83, died in 1975 in Airdrie.

Ian's maternal grandparents – Thomas Miller and Margaret Steel Rogan

Ian's maternal grandfather Thomas Miller was born about 1880 most likely in Lanarkshire and his grandmother Margaret Steel Rogan was born about 1883 also in Lanarkshire to father surnamed Rogan and mother surnamed Nicolson. Thomas Miller, a forge worker, married Margaret Steel Rogan in 1906 and daughter Margaret Steel Rogan Miller was born in 1920 in Coatbridge, Old Monkland. Thomas Miller, a forge manager, was dead by 1948, although, wife Margaret was alive and living at 22 Mitchell Street, Kirkwood, Coatbridge. Margaret Steel Miller nee Rogan, 85, died in 1968 in Coatbridge.

Chapter 17:

Sir Alex Ferguson CBE (Manager)
(East Stirlingshire, Saint Mirren, Aberdeen, Manchester United and Scotland)
(This chapter is also published in Pride of the Jocks by Derek Niven)
Honours at Aberdeen:
1 EUFA Cup Winners Cup
1 EUFA Super Cup
3 Scottish League titles
4 Scottish Cups
1 Scottish League Cup
1 Drybrough Cup
Honours at Manchester United:
2 European Cups
1 EUFA Cup Winners Cup
1 EUFA Super Cup
1 FIFA Club World Cup
1 Intercontinental Cup

13 English League 1 titles
5 FA Cups
4 FA League Cups
10 FA Charity Shields

The young Alex Ferguson

He was born at his grandmother's home at 357 Shieldhall Road, Govan, Glasgow on Hogmanay 1941, during the dark days of WWII. Alexander Chapman Ferguson was born on 31 December 1941 to Alexander Beaton Ferguson, a plater's helper in the Clyde shipbuilding industry, and mother Elizabeth Hardie. He was initially raised at 6 Broomloan Road, Govan in the shadow of Ibrox Stadium and was an avid Rangers supporter, dreaming of one day playing at Ibrox. He grew up in a tenement at 667 Govan Road, Glasgow, where he lived with his parents and younger brother Martin. Ferguson attended Broomloan Road Primary School and Govan High School. After leaving school Ferguson began as an apprentice toolmaker at Remington Rand in Hillington.

He began his football career with Harmony Row Boys Club in Govan, before moving to Drumchapel Amateurs. Ferguson's senior career began as an amateur with Queen's Park, where he made his debut aged 16, moving to St Johnstone in 1960. At St Johnstone he was unable to command a regular place. However, St Johnstone's failure to sign a forward led its manager to select Ferguson for a 1963 match against Rangers, in which he scored a hat-trick. In 1964, Dunfermline Athletic signed him and Ferguson became a full-time professional. The 1965–66 season saw Ferguson notch up 45 goals in 51 games for Dunfermline. Along with Joe McBride of Celtic, he was equal top goal scorer in the Scottish League with 31 goals. In 1967, he joined Rangers for a record transfer fee between two Scottish clubs. He performed well in Europe during his two seasons with the club. However, Ferguson was blamed for a goal conceded in the 1969 Scottish Cup Final, in a match in which he was assigned to mark Celtic captain, Billy McNeill, and he was subsequently forced to play for the club's reserves. According to his brother Martin, Ferguson was so upset by the experience that he threw his losers' medal away. It was claimed that Ferguson suffered discrimination at Rangers after his marriage to Roman Catholic wife Cathy Holding, but he stated that Rangers knew of his wife's religion when he joined the club. He left Rangers reluctantly due to the fall-out from his cup final mistake.

Nottingham Forest wanted to sign Ferguson, but Cathy was not keen, so he went to Falkirk instead. He remained at Brockville for four years and he was promoted to player-coach, but when John Prentice became manager, he removed Ferguson's coaching responsibilities. Ferguson responded by requesting a transfer and moved to Ayr United, finishing his playing career in 1974.

Ferguson the manager

Alex Ferguson is arguably the greatest manager ever to grace British football and he has been rated in the top ten of EUFA all-time greats. It will be a long time before Scotland produces a manager of his calibre again. His record is unparalleled in world football, having won almost every honour available in Scotland, England, Europe and world club levels. The press and the fans nicknamed him 'Fergie', a name that became synonymous with other Ferguson-related metaphors such as the "New Firm", the "siege mentality", the "Class of 92", the "hairdryer treatment" and "Fergie time".

After spells at East Stirlingshire and St Mirren, where he won the Scottish First Division in 1976-77, Ferguson joined Aberdeen as manager in June 1978. He replaced Billy McNeill who was offered the chance to return to Celtic. Although Aberdeen was one of Scotland's major clubs, they had won the league only once before in 1955. Fergie took Aberdeen to heights of success that they could only dream of with great players such as Jim Leighton, Willie Miller, Alex McLeish and Gordon Strachan. Under his management Aberdeen won three Scottish Premier League titles, four Scottish Cups, one Scottish League Cup and a Drybrough Cup. This was capped by Aberdeen's historic 2-1 victory over the mighty Real Madrid on 11 May 1983 in the European Cup Winners' Cup and a European Super Cup win over European Champions Hamburger SV in December 1983. Ferguson was assistant manager for the Scottish national side during qualifying for the 1986 World Cup. Tragically, manager Jock Stein, who Ferguson held in high esteem, had collapsed and died in Cardiff on 10 September 1985, when Scotland qualified for a play-off against Australia. Ferguson agreed to take charge of the Scottish national side against the Australians and subsequently at the World Cup. To allow him to fulfil his international duties he appointed Archie Knox as co-manager at Aberdeen. However, after Scotland failed to progress past the group stages of the World Cup, Alex Ferguson stepped down as national team manager on 15 June 1986.

Ferguson was appointed Manchester United manager on 6 November 1986, but the success he had achieved at Aberdeen appeared to elude him for three long years. In 1989-90, following an early season run of six defeats and two draws, a banner declared: *"Three years of excuses and it's still crap...ta-ra Fergie."* He later described December 1989 as *"the darkest period he had ever suffered in the game"* as United ended the decade just outside the relegation zone. Ferguson later revealed that the board of directors had assured him that they were not considering his dismissal. The 1990 FA cup win is often cited as the match that saved Ferguson's Old Trafford career. United went on to win the FA Cup, beating Crystal Palace 1–0 in the final replay, giving Ferguson his first major trophy as United manager.

Fergie's stellar career at Old Trafford took off and in the next 13 years he steered United to an unprecedented 13 Premier League titles, five FA Cups, four English League Cups, ten FA Charity Shields, two EUFA Champions Leagues, two EUFA Cup Winners' Cups, one EUFA Super Cup, one Intercontinental Cup and a FIFA Club World Cup.

Just days after winning the FA Cup final, United travelled to Barcelona, the setting for the 1999 Champions League final. Ferguson contemplated his team selection against Bayern Munich. Suspensions to Paul Scholes and Roy Keane ruled both players out. David Beckham was positioned in centre midfield, Ryan Giggs was moved to the right wing and Jesper Blomqvist started on the left. Fergie felt these changes would prevent the Germans from playing narrow. However, United conceded in the first six minutes from Mario Basler's free kick.

Teddy Sheringham substituted Blomqvist and he equalised from a corner in the first minute of additional time. Steve McClaren told Ferguson they needed to get the team organised for extra time. Fergie famously replied: *"Steve, this game isn't finished!"* Three minutes into added time Ole Gunnar Solskjær scored an unbelievable winner, which completed an unprecedented treble for United. Ferguson, interviewed moments after, exclaimed: *"I can't believe it. Football, bloody hell. But they never gave in and that's what won it!"*

PRIDE OF THE DONS

Ferguson was knighted by the Queen in 1999 for his services to football. On 8 May 2013, Sir Alex Ferguson announced that he was to retire as manager at the end of the season, but would remain at the club as director and club ambassador. The Guardian announced it was the "end of an era", while UEFA president Michel Platini said that Ferguson was "a true visionary". Prime Minister David Cameron described Ferguson as a "remarkable man in British football".

Alex's parents – Alexander Beaton Ferguson and Elizabeth Hardie

Alex's father Alexander Beaton Ferguson was born on 29 October 1912 at 107 Main Street, Renton, Dunbartonshire to father John Ferguson, a plater's helper, and mother Janet Montgomery Beaton, aka Jenny. The family later moved to 357 Shieldhall Road, Govan and Alexander went to work as a ship plater's helper in the world-famous Govan shipyards. It was in Govan during WWII that he met Elizabeth Hardie, almost 10 years his junior. Alex's mother Elizabeth Hardie was born on 17 January 1922 at 13 Albert Street, Govan, Glasgow to her father Archibald Hardie, a tramcar conductor, and her mother Susan Mansell. After leaving school Elizabeth got a job as a rubber factory worker, possibly in the nearby Dunlop rubber works at Inchinnan.

Alexander Beaton Ferguson, 28, a ship plater's helper, of 357 Shieldhall Road, Govan, married wife Elizabeth Hardie, 19, a rubber factory worker, of No.12 Neptune Street, Govan, on 27 June 1941 at 639 Govan Road, Glasgow. The wedding was conducted by Rev Thomas Notman, minister of Govan St Mary's Church of Scotland; the best man was John Ferguson, Alex's brother, of No.5 Dunvegan Street, and the best maid was Mary Agnes Hardie, Elizabeth's sister, of 12 Neptune Street, Govan. Just five days previously, Hitler launched Operation Barbarossa on the Eastern Front which brought Stalin's Soviet Union into the war. Alex and Elizabeth had two known sons; Alexander and Martin.

Alex's paternal grandparents – John Ferguson and Janet Montgomery Beaton

Alex's paternal grandfather John Ferguson was born on 26 September 1880 at 129 High Street, Dumbarton, to father Robert Ferguson, a journeyman riveter, and mother Catherine Mulholland. In 1891, John, 10, a scholar, resided at 101 High Street, Dumbarton with his parents and siblings. After schooling John went to work in the Dumbarton shipyards, probably with the main shipbuilder in the area, Denny & Co. Within five years John was an orphan as his parents Robert and Catherine both succumbed to the dreaded Victorian killer disease tuberculosis.

Alex's grandmother Janet Montgomery Beaton, aka Jenny, was born around 1890 possibly in Renton, Dunbartonshire, to her father Alexander Beaton, 29, a hammerman, and her mother Isabella Fairley. John Ferguson, a ship plater's helper, of 16 West Bridgend, Dumbarton married Jenny Montgomery Beaton, 22, a printfield worker, of 82 Main Street, Renton, on 23 August 1912 at the Public Hall, Renton. The wedding was conducted by Rev A H Macpherson, officiating minister, United Free Church of Scotland; the best man was George Ferguson, John's brother, and the best maid was Mary McGregor. Son Alexander Beaton Ferguson was born just nine weeks later on 29 October 1912 at 107 Main Street, Renton, Dunbartonshire. John Ferguson, a ship plater's helper, was dead by 1941, however, his wife, who had remarried and was now Janet Miller previously Ferguson nee Beaton was still alive at that time during WWII.

Alex's maternal grandparents – Archibald Hardie and Susan Mansell

Alex's maternal grandfather Archibald Hardie was born around 1896 probably in Glasgow to father Robert Hardie, an iron moulder, and his mother Mary McFarlane. After leaving school Archie became a tramcar conductor at Govan Depot in the once extensive Glasgow Corporation tramway system.

His grandmother Susan Mansell was born around 1899 also probably in Glasgow to father Thomas James Mansell, a quay labourer, and mother Winifred Shields. After schooling Susan got a job as a laundress. Archibald Hardie, 23, a tramcar conductor, of 123 Crookston Street, now named Carnoustie Street, Glasgow, married Susan Mansell, 19, a laundress, at St Saviour's Roman Catholic Chapel, Govan, on 26 September 1919. The wedding was conducted by Fr William Daly; the best man was Alexander Hardie, Archie's brother, and the best maid was Annie Mansell, Susan's sister. Archie and wife Susan had two known daughters in Govan; Elizabeth and Mary Agnes. Daughter Elizabeth Hardie was born on 17 January 1922 at 13 Albert Street, Govan. However, within a couple of years Archie and Susan's marriage irretrievably broke down and unusually for a Roman Catholic marriage of that era it ended in divorce in 1925. Archibald Hardie, a tramcar conductor, and ex-wife Susan Hardie nee Mansell were both still alive in 1941.

Alex's paternal great-grandparents – Robert Ferguson and Catherine Mulholland

Alex's paternal great-grandfather was Robert Ferguson who was born illegitimately on 6 September 1854 in Dumbarton, Dunbartonshire to his father Robert Ferguson, a sawyer, and mother Anne Scullion. Robert was baptised on 8 September by Father R A Wilson in St

Patrick's RC Church in Dumbarton, as recorded in the Catholic Parish Registers as follows: -

CPR Births Dumbarton, St Patrick's
1854: September 8th: Robert natural son of Robert Ferguson & Anne Scullion, born 6th instant, sponsor Sarah Irvine: [Priest] R A Wilson

Robert's father Robert was dead by 1861. In 1861, Robert Ferguson, 7, a scholar, lodged at the home of a widowed Irishwoman named Margaret, 78, at 90 High Street, Dumbarton, with his mother Anna Scullion, 36, a widowed washerwoman, and his brother John, 3. In 1871, Robert Ferguson, 16, a riveter, resided at 152 High Street, Dumbarton with his mother Ann Scullion, 50, still a washerwoman, and his brother John, 12, a rivet heater. Alex's great-grandmother named Catherine Mulholland, born around 1859, probably in Dumbarton, to father John Mulholland, a quarryman, and mother Agnes Hendry. Robert Ferguson, a journeyman riveter, married Catherine Mulholland on 11 July in Dumbarton. Robert and Catherine had five known children in Dumbarton; John (b. 26 September 1880), Mary (b. ~1883), Catherine (b. ~1887), George (b. ~1889) and also Patrick (b. ~1891). Son John Ferguson was born on 26 September 1880 at 129 High Street, Dumbarton.

In 1891, Robert Ferguson, 35, a riveter, resided at 101 High Street, Dumbarton, with wife Catherine, 31, his children John, 10, a scholar, Mary, 8, a scholar, Catherine, 4, George, 2, and Patrick, less than a month old.

Just three years later that terrible Victorian killer tuberculosis (or phthisis) stalked the Ferguson household. Catherine Ferguson, only 35, died on 11 March 1894 at 107 High Street, Dumbarton, of phthisis pulmonalis as certified by Dr William Little MD PhD (Camb). Tragically, the following year in 1895, Robert also contracted tuberculosis and unable to work he was admitted to the Dumbarton Combination Poorhouse at Townend Road. The workhouse was erected on the northern outskirts of the town in 1862 and an infirmary block for up to 60 patients, unfortunately named the lunacy wards, was added in 1866. Robert Ferguson, 40, a pauper and formerly a shipyard riveter, died on 16 May 1896 at the Dumbarton Combination Poorhouse of phthisis pulmonalis as certified by Dr James Wilson LFP&S (Glasgow) and the death was registered by John Henderson, the lunatic warder. Robert Ferguson died a pauper in the poorhouse, but within a few short generations his descendant would become an illustrious multi-millionaire.

The records of the Dumbarton Poorhouse are scant for this period, however, the following report by the Commissioner for the lunacy wards almost certainly confirms the admittance and tragic death of Robert Ferguson, but also gives an insight into the conditions faced by inmates in the infirmary block.

At the Quarterly Meeting of the Dumbarton Combination Poor House Committee held within the Board Room of the Poor House the 13th August 1896 ... A report by Dr John Sibbald, Commissioner in Lunacy, respecting the Condition of the Lunatic Wards of the House and the Inmates thereby, dated the 13th June last, was laid before the Meeting. This Report was also ordered to be engrossed in the Minutes. It is as follows viz: - "Lunatic Wards, Dumbarton Poorhouse, 13th June 1896. There are 29 men and 31 women in the wards as patients at this date. Since 13th January, the date of last visit, one man has been admitted and one man has died. The patients were found in a satisfactory condition. They are suitably clothed, and their food is good and plentiful. All are employed in useful and healthy work except those whose bodily condition makes them unfit. The recommendation in the preceding entry as to the improvement of the bathing and water closet arrangements are here repeated. The books and registers were found regularly and correctly kept." [signed] ....John Sibbald, Commissioner in Lunacy.

Alex's paternal great-grandparents – Alexander Beaton and Isabella Fairley

Alex's other paternal great-grandfather was named Alexander Beaton, and also the likely progenitor of Alex Ferguson's first name, and his great-grandmother was Isabella Fairley, and they were born around 1860, possibly in Dunbartonshire. Alexander, a hammerman, and wife Isabella had a known daughter Janet Montgomery Beaton, aka Jenny (b. ~1890) possibly in Renton, Dunbartonshire. Alexander Beaton, a hammerman, was still alive in 1912, however, his wife Isabella Beaton nee Fairley was dead by that time.

Alex's maternal great-grandparents – Robert Hardie and Mary McFarlane

Alex's maternal great-grandfather was Robert Hardie. His great-grandmother was Mary McFarlane and they were born around 1870 possibly in Glasgow. Robert, an iron moulder, and Mary had two known sons; Archibald, aka Archie (b. ~1896) and Alexander. Robert Hardie, an iron moulder, was dead by 1919, however, his wife, who had remarried, Mary McDonald previously Hardie nee McFarlane was still alive at that time.

Alex's maternal great-grandparents – Thomas James Mansell and Winifred Shields

Alex's maternal great-grandfather Thomas James Mansell and his great-grandmother Winifred Shields were born around 1870 possibly in Glasgow. Thomas, a quay labourer, and Winifred had two known daughters; Susan (b. ~1899) and Annie. Thomas James Mansell, a quay labourer, was dead by 1919, however, his wife, Winifred Mansell nee Shields was still alive at that time.

Alex's paternal great-great-grandparents – Robert Ferguson and Anne Scullion

Alex's paternal great-great-grandfather Robert Ferguson was born around 1820, possibly in Ireland, although this has not been fully confirmed. Alex's great-great-grandmother Agnes Scullion, aka Ann or Anna, was born about 1825 in Ireland and she almost certainly emigrated to Dumbarton to escape the ravages of the Irish Potato Famine (1846-52). Robert Ferguson, a sawyer, co-habited with his common law wife Ann Scullion and they had two known illegitimate sons in Dumbarton; Robert (b. 6 September 1854) and John (b. 20 June 1858). Son Robert was born on 6 September 1854 and baptised on 8 September by Fr R A Wilson in St Patrick's Roman Catholic Church, Dumbarton, as recorded in the Catholic Parish Registers. Son John Ferguson was born on 20 June 1858 in High Street, Dumbarton.

However, Robert Ferguson was dead before 1861 and Ann was left a widow to raise two young boys and she took in people's washing to make ends meet. In 1861, Anna Scullion, 36, a washerwoman, lodged at the home of a widowed Irishwoman named Margaret, 78, at 90 High Street, Dumbarton, with her sons Robert Ferguson, 7, a scholar, and John, 3. Also lodging there was Elizabeth Scullion, 28, a washerwoman, likely to be Ann's younger sister.

In 1871, Ann Scullion, 50, still a washerwoman, resided at 152 High Street, Dumbarton, with her sons Robert Ferguson, 16, a riveter, and John, 12, a rivet heater. Robert and John were most likely employed at the main shipyard in Dumbarton, which was Denny's. Ann Scullion, who never married, was dead by 1896.

Alex's paternal great-great-grandparents – John Mulholland and Agnes Hendry

Alex's other paternal great-great-grandfather John Mulholland and great-great-grandmother Agnes Hendry were born about 1830, probably in Ireland. John, a quarryman probably at Dumbuck Quarry, near Dumbarton, and wife Agnes had a known daughter named Catherine (b. ~ 1859) possibly in Dumbarton. John Mulholland, a quarryman, was dead by 1894, however, his wife Agnes Mulholland nee Hendry was still alive at that time.

Conclusion

First and foremost, this book is a celebration of the achievement of a group of young Scottish lads who, 40 years ago on 11 May 1983, managed by the great Alex Ferguson, achieved the extraordinary feat of winning the European Cup Winner's Cup. They subsequently won the 1983 European Super Cup, the only Scottish side to have lifted two European trophies. Never again in the annals of Scottish football are we likely to see a team with players of humble backgrounds achieve such a feat of sporting excellence.

The family histories of the players wholly underline the humbleness of their ancestral origins. These were men and women who criss-crossed Scotland to scratch a meagre living as agricultural labourers, coal miners, railway workers and domestic servants throughout the Dickensian Victorian era. Poverty-stricken people who emigrated from Ireland to escape famine and destitution in the mid-19th century.

Into the 20th century the family histories tell of the struggle to survive during two devastating World Wars and of the desperate poverty during the global Great Depression of the 1930s. In many ways the family histories of these men and women are no different to our own family histories. Most of us can trace our ancestry back to humble beginnings throughout the Agrarian and Industrial Revolutions.

DEREK NIVEN

What defines this book is the culmination of these specific family histories in producing sixteen remarkable young men who went on to create what was arguably some of the greatest Scottish sporting achievements of the 20th century. In conclusion, this book sets out to celebrate – the Gothenburg Greats.

PRIDE OF THE DONS

Player References

In the Firing Line: The Jim Leighton Story, Jim Leighton and Ken Robertson, 2000

McMaster & Commander: The Business of Winning, John McMaster, Graham Hunter, et al., 2023

The Don of an Era, Alastair Macdonald, Alex McLeish, et al., 1988

The Don: The Willie Miller Story, Willie Miller, 2013

Strachan: My Life in Football, Gordon Strachan, 2006

In Where it Hurts: My Autobiography, Bryan Gunn, 2015

Genealogical References

Statutory Registrations of Births, Marriages and Deaths, Census Records and Old Parish Registers: National Records of Scotland, General Register House, Edinburgh

Statutory Registrations of Births, Marriages and Deaths: General Register Office, London

Familysearch.org

Findmypast.co.uk

FreeBMD.co.uk

Ancestry.co.uk

Association of Scottish Genealogists and Researchers in Archives (ASGRA)

Online and Other References

The Mitchell Library

National Library of Scotland (digital.nls.uk/directories)

ScotlandsPlaces.gov.uk

British Listed Buildings

Scottishshale.org.uk

Scottishmining.co.uk

Dam Dim Tea Estate, Jalpaiguri, West Bengal, India

Dictionary.com

Wikipedia.co.uk

Wikimedia Commons

Surname Database

Canmore

DEREK NIVEN

Glossary of Players' Origin of Surnames

Chapter 1: Leighton – recorded as Layton, Laytoun, Leighton, Leyton and Leaton, this is a famous surname of English or Scottish origins. It is locational from either Leaton or Leighton in Bedfordshire, Cheshire, Huntingdon, Shropshire, or Laytoun in Scotland. All derive from the pre-7th century word 'leac' meaning a leek, and describing leek farms.

Chapter 2: Rougvie – this is a surname of uncertain origin, although it is likely to be derived from Scottish Gaelic and is found predominantly in Fife.

Chapter 3: McMaster – this interesting surname is of Gaelic origin, found in Ireland and Scotland, and is the Anglicized form of the Gaelic name "Mac Maighstir", composed of the Gaelic prefix "Mac", the son of, and "maighstir", master, a cleric, from the Latin "magister".

Chapter 4: Cooper – one of the most important medieval crafts was barrel or tub making. The origin is Anglo Saxon, derived from the German "kuper" itself a derivative of "kup" - a container. The occupational surname of Cooper was first used in England in the 8th century.

Chapter 5: McLeish – this long-established surname is medieval Scottish. It is a developed form of the Old Gaelic Mac Gille Iosa, meaning the son of the servant of Jesus, from 'Mac' meaning son of, 'gille', a follower, and 'Iosa', the Gaelic form of Jesus.

Chapter 6: Miller – this notable surname is Anglo-Scottish. It is an occupational surname, and describes a corn miller, or at least someone in charge of a mill. It originated in the Olde English word "mylene" and later "milne", but ultimately from the Latin word "molere".

Chapter 7: Strachan – this name is of Scottish locational origin, from the lands of Strachan (pronounced "Strawan") in Kincardineshire. The name derives from the Gaelic "strath" meaning a valley, plus "eachain", the plural of "each" a horse, i.e., "the valley of the horses".

Chapter 8: Simpson – a surname of Anglo-Scottish believed to be derived from 'the son of Simon', of biblical origins.

Chapter 9: McGhee – this long-established surname, of Scottish and Irish origin, is an Anglicized form of the Old Gaelic "Mac Aoidh", son of Aodh, from "Mac", son of, and the Celtic male given name Aodh, "fire" or "fire-spring", originally the name of a pagan god.

Chapter 10: Black – this very old surname, popular in Scotland and England, has at least two possible origins, the first being a nickname given by the invading Angles and Saxons to the native Celts and Britons who were darker-haired and darker-skinned than themselves. The second possible origin is an occupational surname as a shortened form of blacksmith.

Chapter 11: Weir – this interesting and unusual name, with variant spellings Wear, Were, Where, etc., derives from a topographical surname for a dweller by a dam, or keeper of a fishing-weir, from the Olde English word "wer", weir, dam, fish-trap.

Chapter 12: Kennedy – this is an anglicized form of an Olde Gaelic (Scots and Irish) personal / nickname 'cinneidigh or cinneide', a compound of the elements 'cinn' meaning 'head', plus 'eide' translating variously as 'grim' or 'helmeted'. Cinneide was the nephew of Brian Boru, High King of Ireland (1002 - 1014), and the surname O' Cinneide came into being in Ireland in the 11th century.

Chapter 13: Gunn – this interesting name has two main derivations. The first is from the Olde Norse Viking pre-7th century personal name "Gunnr", meaning battle. Secondly, a metonymic occupational name for someone who operated a Siege Cannon, from the Medieval word "gunne" meaning a cannon. It could also have been used as a nickname for a person with a forceful temperament.

Chapter 14: Watson – a famous Anglo-Scottish surname of great antiquity. Very popular in the north of England and the borders, it is one of the patronymic forms of the pre-7th century popular male personal name Watt. It is a development of the Anglo-Saxon personal name and later surname, Walter, meaning 'powerful warrior'.

Chapter 15: Hewitt – a name brought to England by the Hewitt family ancestors when they migrated there after the Norman Conquest in 1066. The Hewitt family lived in Huet or Huest near Evreux in Normandy, France. Alternatively, the name was derived from 'the son of Hugh'; Middle English Hugh, How, and Hew, diminutives Hughet and Hewet.

Chapter 16: Angus – this surname has two main origins. Firstly, it may be Scottish / Irish from the Gaelic personal name "Aonghus", composed of the elements "aon" one, plus "ghus" choice; hence "unique choice". It may also be of Scottish locational origin from the East coast county of Angus, with the Gaelic derivation being the same.

Chapter 17: Ferguson – a surname of Old Gaelic origin, found in Ireland and Scotland, and is a patronymic form of Fergus, from the Gaelic personal name "Fearghus", composed of the elements, "fear", man, and "gus", vigour, force, with the patronymic ending "son". This Gaelic personal name was the name of an early Irish mythological figure, a valiant warrior, and was also the name of St. Columba's grandfather.

About the author

Derek Niven is a pseudonym used by the author John McGee, an ASGRA member, in publishing his factual and genealogical writings. Derek Beaugarde is used for his science fiction writings. John McGee was born in 1956 in Corkerhill railway village, Glasgow. He attended Mosspark Primary and Allan Glen's schools. To explain, the late famous actor Sir Dirk Bogarde spent three unhappy years at Allan Glen's as a pupil named Derek Niven van den Bogaerde. The observant reader will readily discern the origin of the two pseudonyms. After spending 34 years in the rail industry in train planning and accountancy John McGee retired in 2007.

In 2012 the idea for his science fiction novel emerged. 2084: The End of Days © Derek Beaugarde was published by Corkerhill Press in 2016. In the years leading up to 2084 seven disparate men and women across the globe battle with their own personal frailties and human tragedies. Suddenly they all find themselves drawn together to fight for survival against the ultimate global disaster – Armageddon! 2084: The End of Days is their story and mankind's future destiny.

Books in the 2084 Trilogy by Derek Beaugarde:

2112: Revelation, Derek Beaugarde © 2022

2048: The Eye of Horus, Derek Beaugarde © 2023

Books in the Pride Series by Derek Niven: -

Pride of the Lions: the untold story of the men and women who made the Lisbon Lions, Derek Niven © 2017

Pride of the Jocks: the untold story of the men and women who made the greatest Scottish managers © Derek Niven, 2018

Pride of the Bears: the untold story of the men and women who made the Barça Bears © Derek Niven, 2020

Pride of the Hearts: the untold story of the men and women who made the Great War heroes of Heart of Midlothian © Derek Niven, 2021

Pride of the Three Lions: the untold story of the men and women who made the heroes of Wembley 1966 © Derek Niven, 2022

Pride of the Red Devils: the untold story of the men and women who made the United heroes of Wembley 1968 © Derek Niven, 2024

PRIDE OF THE DONS